Face to Face is by far one of the greatest books that I have read. The detailed account of several godly men brings the Bible to life. The spirit of the writer comes through with his strong passion and zeal for everyone to experience all God has for him or her. In a day when so many books are being written about the glory of God and His holiness, there are such refreshing accounts of the writer actually experiencing what he has written about. Something has been missing in the lives of so many of God's people as they hurry through day after day doing what is known as "business as usual." This book clearly calls God's people to repentance, heart cleansing, humility, and holiness. As these things happen in our lives, we read about meeting Him "face to face." I highly recommend this book to anyone desiring a closer walk with God or someone who feels something is missing in his or her Christian walk.

—TENA SLOAN

CO-PASTOR AND MISSIONS DIRECTOR

CELEBRATION FAMILY CHURCH

A compelling call to join the chorus of those who have truly known God "face to face"! You will know great characters of the Bible on a level you have never known them before. You will feel the passion they felt to know God on a more personal and intimate level. And you will understand why they were able to experience the depth of His love and the security of His strength. Over the past thirty-five years of ministry, I have read many books that purport to address the subject of knowing God on a more intimate level, and yet this is, without question, the most biblically based treatise on the subject that I have ever encountered. In my travels, I meet many individuals who are longing to know Christ, individuals who are tired of all the common clichés of today's "milk and cookie crowd," people who are prepared to receive the fullness of God's presence. In a time riveting with great spiritual hunger and global confusion about who God really is, Jesse Wilson has captured the biblical key that unlocks the door of understanding how we can be "in the presence of Jehovah"!

—DONNIE W. SMITH, D.MIN.

ADMINISTRATIVE BISHOP

CHURCH OF GOD, FLORIDA

face to face

JESSE WILSON

CREATION
HOUSE PRESS

FACE TO FACE: GOING BEYOND THE VEIL by Jesse Wilson
Published by Creation House Press
A Strang Company
600 Rinehart Road
Lake Mary, Florida 32746
www.creationhouse.com

Unless otherwise noted, all Scripture quotations are from the King James Version of the Bible.

Unless otherwise noted, word definitions and derivations are from *Strong's Exhaustive Concordance of the Bible,* ed. James Strong (Nashville, TN: Thomas Nelson Publishers, 1997).

Cover design by Karen Grindley

Library of Congress Catalog Card Number: 2003115717
International Standard Book Number: 1-59185-463-6

04 05 06 07 08— 987654321
Printed in the United States of America

Acknowledgments

First, I want to thank the One who gave me life abundantly, the One who set me free, my Lover and best Friend, Jesus Christ! I also want to thank my wife for her continual prayers and her unconditional love; you're the best, baby. Thanks to Mary Bradshaw for proofing the original text for scriptural correctness. Special thanks to Tammy Peoples, a true intercessor of God. Your prayers for my wife and me, and your words of encouragement, were timely and inspired; thank you. I also want to give a very special thanks to my pastors, Mike and Tena Sloan. Your mentoring and friendship have meant so much to me. Many people have played a role in my life, none as important as you. Your prophetic messages and counseling have been and still are a great strength to us. Thank you for taking us under your wings and teaching us to expect big things from God! Thank you, Mom, for helping get this project off the ground. You truly are the best mother a person could have, and I love you. Finally, thank you, Celebration Church family! Your aggressive hunger and desire for His presence is contagious! The glory of the latter house will be greater than the former!

Contents

Preface

This book is dedicated to all the hungry people who long for intimacy with the Father, a hunger that goes beyond the ordinary and steps into the extraordinary. It is a call to those who are tired of church as usual and long for something more, something real and exciting. That something is found in the pages of this book; it's a real and close relationship with the Father, the kind of relationship He intended we enjoy when over five thousand years ago, God created man and placed him in the center of the garden. It was never His intention that we fail, but for whatever reason, as is the case today, we find other things to occupy our time rather than fellowshipping with Him. Maybe people think that such a closeness is only reserved for those of the Old and New Testaments. Perhaps we don't think God really desires such a relationship. Or maybe it is because such a relationship, such a closeness, calls for a sacrifice, something unfortunately we in America know very little about. We have been so blessed in this great nation, so blessed with material goods and such an influx of the Word, that we have become complacent.

How it must break the Father's heart to look upon His American bride and see only a shell of what we once were and what we could be again. This book is more than a book about building an intimate relationship with the Father. It's also a call to the church, the American church, to lay aside the distractions, lay aside our sins, and raise the level of our hunger. God wants to shake the nations of the world prior to the return of Christ. He is looking for those who will rise up like Daniel and do exploits for Him. I thank God for the healings we have experienced in our churches. But He is wanting to do more than cure headaches and colds. He wants to raise the dead in our midst; He wants to touch the crippled and maimed so they rise up and walk again! He wants us to be so overcome with His presence that like Peter, our shadow gets lost in His shadow, and people are healed when we walk by. Yet what we call the exception in our churches was called the norm in the early New Testament church. Jesus is coming again (there is no doubt about that), but if He comes now most of His American bride will be left behind. The church was birthed in power and you can be sure that she will be taken in power. We will not go as a whipped dog running with its tail between its legs. Yet that is the case right now; the church is too caught up in the mentality that cries out every Sunday, "What's in it for me?" If you are looking for another "get rich quick" book or a book on how to obtain riches from God, you may want to check some other ministries. This book is for those who are hungry—not hungry for man's inventions and ideas, but a hunger for Him that surpasses every other desire you have. God will use such a hungry person to shake this nation and to shake the world. Are you hungry? Do you want Him more than His blessings? Then I invite you to come into the holy of holies, face to face, beyond the veil.

*"And the Lord spake
unto Moses face to face."*
—Exodus 33:11

CHAPTER 1

Beginning
the Journey

What does it mean to speak with God face to face? I have read Exodus 33:11 many times; each time I could not help thinking that I was missing something in my relationship with God. More recently, I have become convinced of that fact—I have been missing a much closer, more intimate relationship with the Creator of the universe, God Himself, than I dreamed possible.

It was in 1999, while serving as pastor in a small outreach ministry in Dade City, Florida, that I began my journey of drawing closer to God. The Word of God declares that no one can come to Jesus except the Father draws him. (See John 6:44.) Thus I began praying to the Holy Spirit to draw me and give me a deep, consuming desire to know Him more. The scriptures declare this promise: "Draw close to God, and He will draw close to you" (James 4:8, author's paraphrase). The Holy Spirit initiates the desire in our hearts, but it is up to us to act upon that desire—to choose to draw close to God.

Relationship with God bears similarities to our human relationships. For example, when I first saw my wife and she
smiled at me, that was an initial invitation to relationship. But
had I not pursued her, I would not have known the joy of the
past eleven years of marriage. Similarly, I began my pursuit of
God; I longed to know Him in a manner that few have experienced. As I began my journey, it was incredible to begin to
experience His presence in a new way. I would go into the
sanctuary of my small church and pray, "Father, I want to get
as close to You as humanly possible." As I knelt and prayed
and meditated upon His goodness, His grace and His love, His
presence filled the room. He began to speak to me as never
before. Or perhaps He had tried to speak to me before, but
now my heart was prepared, and I heard Him as never before.

During the eight months I served as pastor to the outreach,
we not only experienced growth in numbers, but I grew spiritually beyond what I had ever experienced before. As I continued to seek God in this way, people recognized a difference
in the messages I preached. Instead of just preparing sermons,
I longed to crawl up as a child into my Father's lap, lay my
head on His chest and feel His heartbeat. As a result, my messages were filled with a passion to encourage my people to
draw closer to God. My greatest desire was to have them join
me on my journey to the heart and throne of God.

The closer I drew to God, the more the Holy Spirit
revealed things to me that grieved Him. Because God is holy,
His heart is grieved over all unrighteousness, and the closer
we get to Him, the more He reveals those things that grieve
His heart. As we draw closer, we also become more sensitive
to His great love for us. I was enjoying my walk with God
and learning to hear His voice in a new way. Yet I was still not
satisfied with the level of my relationship with Him; I knew
there was much more to experience and taste of Him, and I
hungered for more. The words of the psalmist expressed my
growing desire for God: "...as the deer pants for water
brooks, so pants my soul for you, O God" (Ps. 42:1, author's
paraphrase).

In March of 2000, we were notified that the outreach would be closing because of financial reasons. The following month the doors were closed and for the next couple of months I continued to seek God, enjoying my communion with Him. But during this transition time in our ministry, my wife and I became friends with people who did not share our love for God. Though they went to church, their lifestyle did not reflect our convictions. Sadly, I must confess that it was during that year, perhaps due in part to our church closing, that we became distracted from our pursuit of God. Our relationship with God came to a virtual stand-still as we chose more selfish pursuits. I can understand how easy it is to lose sight of those things that are really impor-tant when one does not keep his priorities in order.

My wife and I remained active in our home church, teach-ing, singing and laboring for Christ. But it became more a matter of just going through the motions of religious form without sensing any real life or commitment. We were get-ting caught up with our friends and doing things that pleased us rather than doing what pleased the Father. When I look back at that period of my life, it pains and grieves me that I so easily let my communion with the Father die.

Our pastor declared, in January 2001, that this would be a year of restoration. That same month my wife and I attended the funeral of a dear minister friend who had chal-lenged us many times at church with her preaching and in her home with her godly lifestyle. Sitting there at her memo-rial service, as we listened to family and friends talk of her deep relationship with God, we were convicted about our spiritual condition. As effectively as she drew people to God when she lived, she also drew us in her death. We were chal-lenged to abandon all to God and to pursue Him with our whole hearts. Sitting in that church in La Belle, Florida, my wife and I determined to seek after God. We would not let friends or family or selfish pursuits distract us any longer.

Yes, it was a difficult decision for us to leave our friends. We knew, however, if we were to enjoy God's closeness and intimacy once again, we needed to remove any and all obstacles. My desire to walk with Him in close communion was greater than my fleshly desires, and I burned inside to feel His heartbeat once again.

It is important to emphasize that, during our period of drifting away from intimate relationship with God, the Holy Spirit never left us. Every time we set foot in church He would convict us. The Holy Spirit never stopped calling us and tugging on our hearts. It was we who had willfully chosen to distance ourselves from Him. We were keeping the level of our relationship with Him where we were comfortable, not at the level the Holy Spirit desired. He wanted all of our hearts, but we were willing to let Him have only a small portion of our hearts and our lives at the time. I am so thankful that the Holy Spirit never stopped wooing us. That is the heart of our heavenly Father: He longs so much for intimate communion with His creation that He never stops drawing.

We were living our pastor's declaration that the year 2001 would be a year of restoration. Little did I know that God was about to take me on a journey that would forever change my relationship with Him. I cannot pinpoint the exact time and place in which I really began to sense new hunger for God, but I know that in 2001 I was gripped with the realization that certain Old and New Testament saints experienced a relationship with God that surpassed what I and many of today's Christians have experienced. I can probably count on one hand the internationally known ministers who have come close to that level of relationship. But even for them, when we compare their lives and ministry, not one of them matches up to an Enoch or a Moses or an Isaiah.

One day as I was praying I said, "Father, I am jealous of the level of relationship with You enjoyed by some of the saints whose lives are recorded in Your Word. I want what they had. I want to hear Your voice with the same clarity that they heard it." Every day, as I took a walk on my lunch break at work, I prayed this prayer. I declared my disappointment in where I was with the level of intimacy with God in my life.

Over and over, I reminded Him of my jealousy of the early saints I was reading about. They heard His voice with such clarity! They had such an incredibly deep intimacy with Him! And God responded to my prayer; He gently reminded me that I was as close to Him as I desired to be. He had initiated the pursuit of relationship with me, but I was the one who determined how far and how deeply our relationship would develop. Hebrews 11:6 says, "He is a rewarder of those who diligently seek after Him" (author's paraphrase). After a few weeks of beseeching God to bring me to a place where I would hear Him with more clarity, He responded. He started speaking to me more clearly. Or, perhaps, I was just listening more; nevertheless, my relationship with God was growing. And I became consumed with a desire to draw closer to Him.

As when I had sought Him earlier, the closer I drew to Him, the more He began to require of me. The Holy Spirit started convicting me of some of my attitudes. Television shows that I used to enjoy, I could not watch anymore. I would hear the Holy Spirit say, "No more, son, that has to go if you want My presence." If you really hunger for only Him and desire Him above anything else, there are some things in your life that He is going to require you to give up or lay aside. Paul wrote in Hebrews 12:1 that we should lay aside every weight and sin which besets or distracts us. The things that the world has to offer are distractions, and nothing more. There is no good thing in the world that can satisfy our hunger for God. God wants us to be enamored with Him and to find that place of fellowship with Him that cannot be matched by any other person or thing. Some things He asks us to lay down because their influence is destructive or sinful. Other things He asks us to lay down may be (or may appear to be) good, but may simply waste our time and energy. Some things He asks us to lay aside may seem insignificant; but doing so offers us the opportunity to exercise our obedience to Him and show our love and honor for Him.

The Word of God makes it clear that we should do things

that edify and strengthen our relationship with God. Paul wrote in Romans 12:1–2, "I beseech you therefore, brethren, by the mercies of God, that ye present your bodies a living sacrifice, holy, acceptable unto God, which is your reasonable service. And be not conformed to this world: but be ye transformed by the renewing of your mind, that ye may prove what is that good, and acceptable, and perfect, will of God." Anything that does not edify or strengthen our relationship with God, but instead promotes a lifestyle and mentality contrary to what the Word teaches, needs to be purged from our lives. We have become so spoiled in our nation with all the amusements available to us that many have lost the ability to just turn everything off and fellowship with God.

Do not think that I—or anyone else who has begun the pursuit of His presence—has attained an exalted position with God. Some people are just hungrier than others for the presence of God, and God rewards that hunger! To satisfy that hunger, some are willing to lay aside all distractions, which are in some cases sin, in order to have more of Him. As was ordained for the tribe of Levi, God wants to be our portion; our inheritance. (See Deuteronomy 18:2.) He longs for us to fall so in love with Him that everything else we value pales in comparison to Him.

Some might ask, "Why go deeper with God? Why move beyond where I am in my relationship with Him?" My answer is, "Why not?" How can anyone walk with God and not have a desire to know Him more intimately? As with any relationship, our relationship with God should mature and grow deeper. The problem with many people is that they are satisfied with going to church three times a week. Then they live their lives the way they want to the rest of the week, without a thought of God. But praise God, there is a call going forth in the Spirit that is being heard by hungry people. It is a call to step out from the mundane into the exciting; to forsake the mediocre and to reach for the vibrant reality of intimacy with God.

As for myself, I am tired of running around His feet, getting a little revelation or insight every once in awhile. I want to crawl up in His lap, lay my head on His chest and feel His heartbeat! I want to hear Him whisper to me and to share things with me. When I step behind the pulpit, I no longer want to just give a "good word"; I want to be ablaze with His anointing and presence! I long to share His heart, not just give facts about Him. I believe that is what preaching is supposed to be!

Good preaching is not lacking in this country; however, what is lacking is the power in our preaching. The reason so many are impressed with what we say rather than what is behind the message is because we have mastered the techniques of preaching. What we have not mastered is sitting in His presence. Maybe that explains why no one's shadow is healing the sick as it did in Peter's day. (See Acts 5:14-15.) Notice the "headlines" in the book of Acts when a few Spirit-empowered men set out to win their world: "These men are turning the world upside down" (Acts 17:6). I did not grow up in church; I do not come from a long line of preachers. In fact, I am the first preacher in my family (from either side). In my sixteen years of being in the church, I have been privileged to attend some well-known Bible schools and have met a number of God's choice servants, yet I have never seen a "headline" like that of Acts 17:6.

We pride ourselves on being able to articulate the Word in such a way that it impresses people. Yet our world is still going to hell! The early church struck fear in those outside the church; today we are ridiculed. Unfortunately, the only headlines we can seem to muster is which minister is running off with the church secretary or which priest or pastor has been abusing a child! We need God's presence in our lives today more than ever. We have tried to do it on our own, and it does not work. In 1 Corinthians 2:4, Paul said, "My speech and my preaching were not with enticing words of man's wisdom, but in demonstration of the Spirit and of power." We have learned to have church without God;

without seeing His power manifest and knowing His presence. But that is about to change. God is calling His own to begin to seek after Him with their whole hearts! He is calling them to set aside everything to be with Him! As many answer the call, God will respond and draw near to them, once again manifesting His power and presence in our churches.

As my pursuit of intimacy with God continued, God began to speak to me through His Word, and I began to examine the lives of those who attained a deeper walk with Him. Remember Mary and Martha? When Jesus stopped in as He usually did, Martha and her sister Mary would treat our Lord to a good meal. On one particular occasion, recorded in Luke 10, Martha was rushing about getting things ready and straightening up the house. Mary, though, was sitting at the feet of Jesus taking in every word that dripped from His mouth. When Martha complained, Jesus' response went beyond the outward realm and right to the heart of the matter. Jesus did not minimize the importance of housework, but the issue with Martha went deeper. She was overly concerned with external things and was ignoring the more important issues of the inner life. In other words, Martha was anxious and distracted about everything. The word *anxious* literally means to be "troubled with cares."

Have you ever met a person who just could not seem to slow down and enjoy life? They always seem to be negative about everything. They never take the time to look at something from a different, more positive perspective. When Martha told Jesus to have Mary help her, her request was birthed out of an inner anxiety, not out of a genuine need for help. Jesus said, "Martha, Martha, you are worried and troubled about many things, but one thing is needed. Mary has chosen that good part, which will not be taken away from her" (Luke 10:41–42, author's paraphrase). Mary had found the cure for being so caught up and distracted over everything. That cure was learning to rest at Jesus' feet.

People who are troubled and distracted by life tend to turn a normal situation into something larger than it really is.

They are so caught up with the cares of life that the smallest issues become magnified. As a result, they become even more anxious and troubled. Thus begins a vicious, never-ending cycle of worry. Mary, though, had found something better; it was listening to the words of the Master. His words calmed her! While thinking on this passage the other day, the Lord spoke to me and said, "It was not the good food that caused Me to always stop and visit with Mary and Martha. It was their love and hunger for Me."

The apostle John tells us in John 12:3 that it was Mary who, six days before the Lord's crucifixion, brought an alabaster box and poured the contents on Jesus' head. She then walked around in front of Him, knelt down at His feet and anointed them with the oil. Some of those sitting at the table with Jesus became upset with her—and with the Lord for allowing her do so—but neither Mary nor Jesus cared what they thought. Such was Mary's love for Jesus, the Man to whose words she clung, the Man who impacted her life so dramatically. It was this same Mary, who along with Mary Magdala, was the first to see Him after His resurrection.

Can you sense His desire for you? A few people really found an intimate relationship with the Lord while He walked this earth—they learned the way to His heart. Mary of Bethany was one of those; another was John, the beloved disciple, whom we will visit in a later chapter. Mary loved Jesus more than anyone or anything. It is that kind of love that Jesus is seeking from us. Total abandonment to Him is saying there is something more important than housework, more important than friends and family, and that something is feeling the Master's heartbeat.

When our relationship with Christ is ablaze, all other relationships will be kept in the right perspective. I wish you could feel what I feel for Him. No, I wish you could feel more than what I feel for Him. He is calling you, beckoning you to draw closer, to come into His presence where your only focus is Him. And you know what? You are His only focus, too. When you are at His feet, you have His full, undivided attention. How He longs to speak with you, to share the things that He has on His heart for you. You may be thinking, *Why would God want to speak with me? I am not a minister.* Or maybe you are a minister, but you are serving out in the middle of nowhere to a small group of people, and you wonder, *How could He have time for me?* God loves all of His children more than we can imagine.

God longs to restore every believer to a place of intimate fellowship with Him. You and I were created for one thing. Contrary to what many have believed and even taught, we were not created for the sole purpose of worshiping Him. God created the angels for that. You and I were created to have fellowship with Him. Heaven is going to be more than standing around with our hands raised, worshiping for eternity. There is more to our relationship than worship. It is my belief that my life is worship unto Him because worship is the result of my fellowship and communion with Him. It is singing love songs to Him and loving Him with all my heart. It is like dating; you sing songs to the one you are pursuing. That is very similar to our worship of God. We are singing and adoring Him; therefore, if I walk in fellowship with Him, then my whole life becomes and is worship unto Him. The Holy Spirit told me one day, "Worship births intimacy, and intimacy births worship. Worship without relationship is just dead ritual." The Father is restoring His bride back to a place of intimacy with Him.

For so many years people have come to church looking for the meaning of life. They want to know the purpose of their existence. We have told them, "You must get saved, then after that you should come to church three times a week and read your Bible, and when you die, you will go to heaven. Once in heaven, you will spend eternity worshiping and praising God." If this is the extent of our teaching, we have missed it, and we are living beneath what God intended for us.

If you are still reading this book, it is because you are hungry. You have been feeling that tugging at your heart! You know that God is drawing and wooing you to come closer to His heart! If you are looking for more "head" knowledge, you will not find it by reading this book. My heart's desire is to lead you into His presence, to help you become even hungrier than you are right now until you are consumed with the desire to know God more intimately. I am not presuming that I have experienced more of His presence than others have; I am only saying that what I have tasted of His presence makes me desperate for more. And I want to share with everyone what little insight God has given me about pursuing intimacy with Him and coming to a place of spending time alone with Him. I can say confidently: "Oh, taste and see that the LORD is good" (Ps. 34:8). Because God longs for intimate communion with everyone, I long to share something, anything, that would birth in you that hunger for Him. This relationship with God is not just for pastors or people we consider to be "super" spiritual, or giants of the faith; It is for every child of God.

I am determined that when I get to heaven and meet God, I am not going to be surprised; I will already know Him. I know that my fellowship with Him now will better prepare me for eternity. When I was in Bible college, I was taught a lot of facts and knowledge about the Word, but not much *about* relationship with the Author. You can know about someone without ever knowing that person. The good news is that we can know God—personally and intimately! My purpose in writing this book is not to share things *about* Him; I want to introduce you to Him. Then I want to leave you two alone to get to know one another better. Do you hear Him calling? He is saying, "Come; come beyond the veil into My presence where it is all about Me."

As we'll study later, the veil was that part of the tabernacle that separated the ark of the covenant and the very presence of God from people. But there were a few people, those who found a way to the Father's heart and into His presence. They didn't have to enter the tabernacle. They entered His presence right where they abode; thus in a sense they did indeed find a way beyond the veil into His presence.

Over the next few chapters we are going to look at the lives of some of those who have gone beyond the veil to meet Him. Not even all the saints written about in the Old and New Testaments have gone beyond the veil, but there were some who did. They had extraordinary relationships with God. Their experiences of touching the eternal teach us something about the Father. I want to know what that is. Don't you?

"And the Lord took the man and put him in the Garden of Eden to care for it…"

—GENESIS 2:15, AUTHOR'S PARAPHRASE

CHAPTER 2

ADAM

Life In the Garden

T he Holy Spirit told me not long ago, "What started in the garden with Adam, Jesus finished in the garden to bring us back to a garden relationship." Think about the Garden of Eden for a moment. God created the most beautiful place and set man in the center of it. He said, "Here, it is all yours. Enjoy it." Had Adam not fallen, we would be living in utopia right now. We would be enjoying God's presence and the good things He placed on earth. Notice that when God created Adam, He did not tell Adam to bow and worship Him. God's purpose for creating man was for fellowship with Him.

The garden, itself, represents that place of intimacy with God—a place of peace and aloneness with Him. It is different with the angels; they also are created beings, but with different responsibilities than what man was responsible for in the garden. Some are warring angels; others do nothing more than worship God. Still others serve as guardians. Unlike the angels, you and I were created in His image. We were created to walk with God. His purpose in creating us, as seen in the garden, was to commune with Him. Being made in His image puts mankind on a higher plain than the angels. Psalm 8:5 says that He made man a little lower than the angels. The original Hebrew text is better translated "a little lower than God." Since angels are not made in His image, mankind is on a higher level with God than the angels.

Being made in His image does not in any way make us equal with God. It does, however, place us in a special relationship to Him. God holds us dear to His heart. Into what other creature did God breathe the breath of life so that he became a living soul? It was David who said, "I am fearfully and wonderfully made" (Ps. 139:14). Why is this important? It is necessary for us to understand that God uniquely created us so that we can fellowship and commune with Him on a level higher than any of His other creations. Because we have the ability to comprehend Him, to hear Him speak and to talk intelligently with Him, He wants us to interact with Him in intimate relationship.

Can you imagine that God—who is everywhere, who knows and sees all—would come down from His throne to personally walk with Adam and Eve in the cool of the day? The Scripture indicates that this was a frequent occurrence (Gen. 3:8–9). This tells me that in the garden God would concentrate His manifest presence in such a way as to be tangibly felt and visibly seen. In the Hebrew the word for "glory" is *kabowd,* which means the heavy, weighty presence of God. This divine presence is different from God's omnipresence that is everywhere at all times. God's manifest presence is different in that it can be felt and, at times, even seen. Those who enter His manifest presence often fall on their faces in reverence and awe for what they see and feel.

It was God's manifest presence that walked with Adam in the garden. Christ came to restore that relationship to mankind. Yes, the Word teaches us that we are to walk by faith and not by sight. And we cannot always trust our feelings; however, when God comes in His concentrated, manifest presence, you will feel His presence! Adam knew when

He was near. He felt Him; he talked with Him; we can even imagine he laughed with Him in sheer joy and delight. I long for such a relationship with God as Adam experienced.

In Genesis 11:5 we find another example of God's manifest presence. When the tower of Babel was being built, the Word says, "The Lord came down to see the city and tower, which the children of men built" (author's paraphrase). As the omniscient (all-knowing) God, He knew what they were building. He could have stayed on His throne and checked it out, yet He came personally to see this abomination. On another occasion, when the sins of Sodom and Gomorrah grieved God, He came to earth personally to look into it, talking with His servant Abraham about what He was going to do. (See Genesis 18.) Each time the scriptures record that God "tangibly" appeared on the earth, some major event took place.

In the garden, He walked with Adam and Eve. They were able to feel His presence, to literally hear Him and commune with God Himself. Are you jealous yet? Why should we settle for less? Why should we accept just going through life without ever knowing God in a real and intimate friendship? Why should we settle for less? We were created for more! God yearns to have relationship with us. For myself, I refuse to settle for less. As I studied the life of Adam, I cried, "Father, this is what I long for!" The Father also longs for this intimate friendship with His creation.

One of the saddest verses in the Bible is found in Genesis 3: "Adam and Eve hid themselves from the presence of the Lord" (v. 8, author's paraphrase). Their sense of separation from God because of their sin broke God's heart because of His love for them and His desire for their companionship. Since that time, God continues to call those who want to know God. He beckons them to come and enter into His presence and walk with Him. Had Adam not fallen through disobedience to God's command, we would be living in a much different world. It is hard to imagine what life was like in the garden for Adam—perfect weather, perfect health, and never growing old, never experiencing any pain or heartache. All this will be restored to us when we join our Lord in heaven.

If you think heaven is going to be boring, you will be surprised. We are not going to be standing around for eternity just praising God. Yes, we will praise and worship Him. Some people believe the myth that we will be sitting on clouds strumming on our harps and singing. Looking at Adam's life in the garden proves otherwise. The Word says, "Eye has not seen, nor ear heard, neither has entered into the heart of man the things God has prepared for them who love Him" (1 Cor. 2:9, author's paraphrase). Jesus said in John 14:2, "I go to prepare a place for you." In that same verse, Jesus stated that there were many mansions in heaven. The Greek word for *mansions* means a dwelling place. We will dwell and live with God in unbroken fellowship.

From what the scripture tells us we know that the garden was beautiful, but the Holy Spirit said to me, "Do not think that God outdid Himself when He created the garden, Jesse. Heaven is so much more beautiful than anything you can possibly imagine." When I think of the garden, I visualize Adam and God spending hours together, just talking and laughing. You may be thinking, "Come on, Jesse. I cannot imagine God laughing and talking with me." Yes, that is the kind of fellowship He desires. Do you hear Him calling you? He is saying, "Come into the garden where we will walk together and laugh—where I will share My heart with you."

If you want to understand this more fully, read the Song of Solomon. We get a perfect picture of the relationship God wants to have with us. How do we get from where we are to where He is? We get there by hungering after Him, by pouring our soul out to Him. I compare it to pursuing a boyfriend or girlfriend. First, you make your intentions or your love known to them. Then you pursue them by doing things that get their attention. It is just the same with God. The only difference, as I explained in the last chapter, is that God initiates this desire. The Holy Spirit places the longing in our heart—not just for salvation, which is the first step, but also for intimate relationship with Him. How we respond to that longing will determine whether or not we experience a "garden" relationship with the Lord.

It may be easier for women than it is for men to grasp the concept of a garden experience. Women seem to understand the emotional side of intimacy better, while men are more prone to grasp the physical side of intimacy. Since I am not a psychologist, I will not spend much time on these gender differences; however, it is important that we understand they exist. The fact is, women may more easily grasp the intimate friendship that God longs to have with us than men do. So to the men I would say, our macho attitude must die if we are to enjoy the intimacy of God's presence. If necessary, we must become in our minds like little boys once again as we approach God. I remember as a young boy I would crawl up in my step-dad's lap to watch television with him. We would go fishing on the weekends and play outside together. While it is true that some men find it easy to come into God's presence and weep or lie before Him and sing out love songs, this is not the experience for many men. Sadly, in many churches, it is the women who experience this intimacy with God while the men stand off in the distance. In the Garden of Eden, there is nothing in Scripture to indicate that either Adam or Eve found it difficult to fellowship intimately with God.

One of the things that makes the church we currently attend different from many churches is the way the men freely relate to each other. We regularly meet to fellowship together. The barriers that society has placed on men's relationships are being torn down. We are not afraid to openly talk about personal issues and struggles. We pray with one another; we cry with one another; we even hug one another. This unique, brotherly relationship with other men is not only helping us support and encourage one another; it is also helping many of us to drop our masculine reserve in our relationship with God. In our church, you will see many of our men dancing freely before God. You will see them bow and weep before the Lord as they worship Him.

The beautiful picture of life in the garden, before the Fall, teaches that God wants to lead each of you to a place where it is just God and you. Adam, no doubt, thoroughly enjoyed his times with the Lord. That is the place where I want to be. The question is, "Are you living it? Are you living in the garden, or have you been there yet?" Once you visit and reach that level of intimate fellowship and communion with God, you will never again want to go back to having a mediocre relationship with Him. In fact, you will begin to long for Him so much that you will eventually begin to tell Him, "Father, I cannot wait to spend eternity in Your presence. I just want to be with You." You will come to a place where you are no longer enthralled with this world or its many distractions, which are often disguised as pleasures. In the garden, it is all about Him! While others are doing their best to survive in this world, you will be so caught up in Him that you will hardly notice the pain of this world.

In the next chapter we will introduce a Bible character who was so in love with God that while out walking with Him one day, he decided that he did not want to come back. He did not want to leave God's presence and spend another waking moment in this sin-filled, crazy world.

Are you hungry for God yet? Can you hear Him calling you from the "garden"? I can hear Him; He is saying, "Where are you, My daughter? Where are you, My son?"

"Enoch walked with God;
and he was not,
for God took him."

—GENESIS 5:24

CHAPTER 3

ENOCH

Walking With Him

The Bible does not tell us much about this man, Enoch. We know that, generationally, he was the seventh from Adam. Jude tells us that Enoch spoke out against the sin of his generation and that Enoch prophesied about the coming of the Lord (Jude 14–15). This gives us insight into the depth of Enoch's relationship with God. As we will find out in later chapters, God shares His heart, His purposes and His plans with those who walk close to Him.

Though Enoch does not leave us much information about his life, what we do know inspires our imagination. When you consider the length of Adam's life (930 years, according to Genesis 5:3), it is very possible that Enoch may have known him. Can you imagine what it would have been like for Enoch to talk to Adam? I can hear him now, "Great, great, great, great, great grandfather, tell me again about the Garden of Eden!" I am certain that Adam's heart still felt the traumatic effects of having been removed from the garden. I'm sure he still agonized over his decision to disobey God; however, something he said must have gotten Enoch's attention because years later we are told that Enoch began a walk with God—a fact which makes people who hunger for God jealous. We are told that Enoch began his incredible journey with God when he was about sixty-five years of age. Genesis 5:21–22 says, "And Enoch lived sixty and five years, and begat Methuselah. And Enoch walked with God after he begat Methuselah three hundred years, and begat sons and daughters." The scripture plainly states that, after Enoch walked with God for hundreds of years, the day came when God just took him home: "Enoch walked with God; then he was no more, for God took him away" (Gen. 5:23–24, author's paraphrase). I believe Enoch woke up that morning, got alone with God, as was his custom, and while basking in God's presence said, "Father, I do not want to leave Your presence. I want to be where You are." And God answered that prayer.

There have been times in my experience that God's presence was so sweet, I can honestly say that I did not want to leave it. There is a place in God where you would rather be with Him than anyone else—or anyplace else, for that matter. If it were not for my wife and children and the pain they would experience, as well as the understanding that, as a minister, I have a divine destiny to fulfill, I would ask the Lord to take me home now! Once that work is completed, I will be free to go to be with God. If the Lord were to take everyone before their appointed time, much would be left undone and millions of people could be lost without a knowledge of God.

The good news, according to the Scriptures, is that we can experience a deep, intimate relationship with the Father right now. We do not have to wait until we get to heaven or until He returns to take us home. Even so, the Father loves to hear us tell Him how much we long to be with Him where He is—just as I love to hear my six-year-old daughter tell me, "Take me with you, Dada!" or to have my twelve-year-old son want to ride to the store with me. Even if I had planned on going alone, I usually take them with me for the pleasure of their company. In the same way, I believe Enoch came to the place of such hunger and desire to be with God that he did not look back, and the Father said, "Okay, come on."

In Jude 14 we are told that Enoch prophesied of the return of the Lord with ten thousands of His saints. That is the one thing we will discover as we look at the lives of those who went beyond the ordinary and entered into deep communion with God: God revealed His heart to them—sharing not only things about Himself or pertaining to their lives, but also His purposes and plans for things to come. In this same way, it still amazes me that I can read a scripture over and over, then suddenly, while alone with God or just talking with Him, He will give me a deeper understanding of its true meaning. I must emphasize that if you are not a minister or in ministry in any capacity, that does not mean that you are not qualified to receive His revelations or insights. God does not speak or show things only to His ministers. As a minister, He may lay a word on my heart for my church or for a church where I am a guest speaker; however, God speaks to all those who are listening. He answers and speaks to hungry people. The life of Enoch shows us that very clearly. Enoch was not a prophet or a minister. He was an ordinary person who hungered for God, and God met him. Although Enoch was ordinary in the sense of being an individual, his walk with God was far from ordinary. That is what Enoch's walk with God teaches us. Anyone can have an extraordinary walk with Him. God does not use extraordinary people as we think of when we look at the great men and women of our day. God uses people who have an extraordinary relationship with Him.

It is simply a reality that not every man or woman of God who ministers from the pulpit today is walking in intimate relationship with God. If you are like me, you enjoy listening to a variety of different ministers. My favorites are those who are obviously living so close to God that when they speak, I sense it is God speaking through them. These ministers are not concerned with popularity or pleasing everyone. They have been with the Lord, and they have something to say. You can tell the difference between a person who just came from the throne room and one who just came out of the front room. There are degrees of relationship with God, just as there are in our human relationships. For example, the level of intimacy I share with my wife is much deeper than even the intimate friendships I have with people in the church I attend.

One time while I was praying in the sanctuary of the church in which I was pastoring, I told the Lord that I did not want to preach anything that was simply from my intellect; I only wanted to speak the truths that were found in Him, birthed by His Spirit. Unfortunately, I did not hold to that conviction. After ministering awhile, I became aware of the phrases and scriptures that seemed to "move" people. And I preached for their response, instead of depending on God for the truth of His Word. Some of us get to the place where we do not depend upon God as much as we once did; we become complacent and think that we know it all. We see this same condition affecting the early church in the first centuries after Christ's ascension. The church was birthed in a blaze of glory when the Holy Spirit fell on those in the upper room. (See Acts 2.) History records that only a few years after the early church fathers—those disciples who walked with Christ—had passed away, the church was no longer depending on the hand of God. Instead they depended upon themselves; therefore, the supernatural power manifestations in the second and third century were far less evident than those in the first century, when the church was birthed.

As modern-day Christians, we can fall into the same trap. We come to rely on our knowledge about God rather than relying upon Him, and then we have the audacity to question why we battle with doubt and unbelief. Today many Christians fight fear, depression, rejection and a host of other demonically influenced states. The primary reason for these bondages is that we have not maintained our intimacy with God. Although it is true that some people suffer depression due to physical illness, our awesome God can also heal them as they seek to dwell in His wonderful presence.

When we look at Enoch, we do not see any variance in His walk with God. His walk was consistent; it was intimate; it was constant! We would have fewer divorces in the church, fewer depressed Christians, and less tolerance for sin if we, like Enoch, had a vibrant, active relationship with God. As I mentioned, Jude tells us that Enoch spoke out against the sins of his generation. (See Jude 15.) Historically, Enoch spoke these prophecies just a few years before Noah came on the scene, and God pronounced His judgment on all humanity.

What would Enoch say today about our generation? What would be his warnings to the ministers who are supposed to be representing God and walking in close fellowship with Him, yet who are leaving their wives for their secretaries? What would he say to the countless numbers of Christians who say they love God, yet rebel against God's delegated authority or who profane the name of God?

As you walk with God and continually enter into His presence, you will become sensitive to His voice. You will come to know what grieves His heart. Just as you know what hurts people's feelings, you will become familiar with the things God hates and over which He grieves. And, you may find yourself speaking out against injustice. A word of caution, however; when speaking out, you must be careful to do so in love and according to God's timing. There have been many times when I was witnessing for the Lord, but not under His direction, and I was nearly martyred or beat up for the cause of Christ! It is important that we do all things according to His direction and timing.

That is not to say that a person will never suffer for the cause of Christ; that has and does happen. But we must be sure to always follow the leading of the Spirit, not just jump into a situation without His clear guidance, otherwise the suffering that might entail could be more our doing than the result of the Word being persecuted.

What does Enoch's walk with God teach us? First, that God takes ordinary people and leads them into an extraordinary relationship with Him, if they are willing. Enoch also teaches us that this walk is to be so exciting and alive that you no longer are subject to this world's strong pull. Your greatest desire will be to walk with God the Father in His world.

Are you jealous yet? Do you hear God calling? He is saying, "Come, walk with me, My daughter, My son. I have many things to share with you." Are you longing for that intimate relationship with God? He is longing for that love relationship with you.

The question that must be answered is this: "Are you willing to pay the price for such a relationship with the Father?" Ordinary people who have an extraordinary walk with God have paid the price for such a relationship. As you will see in the following chapters, you cannot have any other lovers when Christ becomes the Lover of your soul. Exodus 34:14 says, "For the LORD, whose name is Jealous, is a jealous God." When you walk with Him, He wants all of you. That is why Christ said in Luke 14:26 that unless a person hates his mother, father, brothers, sisters, wife and children, he cannot be His disciple. Jesus was not advocating hatred for those with whom we are in these natural relationships; He plainly taught us to love one another. He was speaking of prioritizing our relationships. So great will be our love for Him that, in comparison, all other loves would seem like "hatred." We can, and will, have many friends and loves, but only one lover. It is just as in a marriage—we have one lover, but many family members and friends whom we love to different degrees. It is not hard to gaze at our Lord and at the same time to share a life with our spouse and children, if our relationship priorities are right. God desires to be number one in our lives. He wants to sit upon the throne of our hearts, which is His rightful place.

So how far do you want to go with God? What price are you willing to pay? He paid it all to bring you back to the garden, to bring you back into intimate, personal relationship with Him. Will you, like Enoch, declare, "I'm going to walk with God every day"? Are you hungry yet?

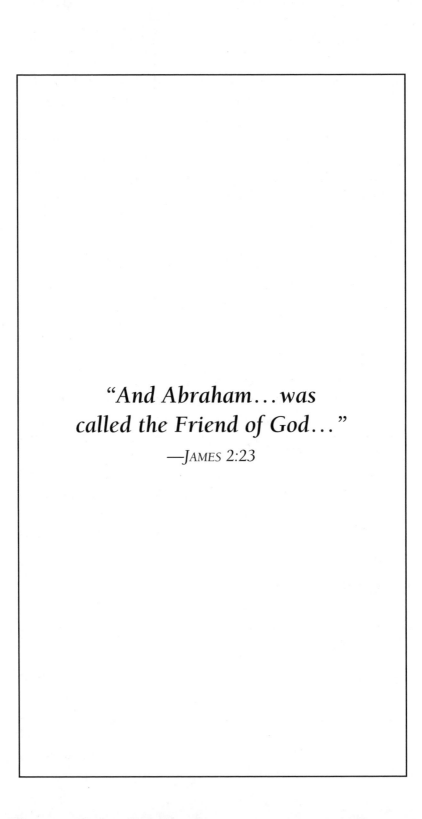

*"And Abraham…was
called the Friend of God…"*

—JAMES 2:23

CHAPTER 4

ABRAHAM

God's Friend

The apostle James referred to Abraham as the friend of God. What a commendation he gave to someone he had never met personally but would have known about only through Scripture. Abraham's life was an exciting one. To leave a legacy of being a friend of God is an incredible testimony. Like Adam and Enoch before him, Abraham knew God in a way that few did. He enjoyed an intimate friendship with God, according to the words of the prophet Isaiah. (See Isaiah 41:8.)

Abraham is one of the most interesting people in the Old Testament. It was to him that God would speak one day, directing him to get away from his family and friends, to "a land that I will show you" (Gen. 12:1). As we read about Abraham's life, we see one thing he does over and over again: he builds altars to God. At that time, these places of surrender were Abraham's chief means of communing and worship to the Father. In fact, Abraham's life is marked by altars, which represented his communion and fellowship with God.

Worship and communion with God is imperative if we are going to move beyond the ordinary into the extraordinary. There is a vast difference between those who go to church and learn *about* God, and those who move beyond that head knowledge into a closeness of knowing Him. Abraham's family knew about God. As descendants of Noah's son, Shem, they would have heard of God's mighty acts. The fact that Abraham, called Abram at that time, did not question the voice of God or His instructions, shows that he must have known about God, but did not know God. Unlike others, however, Abram had a desire to go beyond just knowledge. He wanted to get to know the Person behind the acts, behind the voice.

As he was commanded, Abram left all and went. One of the first things he did was build an altar and call upon God. We do not know how much knowledge of God Abram had prior to this, but he apparently knew that one way to get in touch with Him was to build an altar and worship Him there. From the stories passed down to him, Abraham knew that God would respond to intimate worship, so he built an altar and called upon God.

God's call to walk with Him goes out to every person, but the level and the intensity of the pursuit is entirely up to the individual. God calls not only those whom He knows will come after Him with all their hearts; He also calls all who will hear. Of course, He knows those who will come after Him with a holy and hungry pursuit once they have tasted of His presence. What is interesting about the Word is that God recorded those who rejected Him as well as those who accepted Him. The Word also records those who, like Adam, Enoch and Abraham, walked with God in such an awesome fellowship and communion that it makes those of us who are hungry for Him jealous! You will hear me repeat this statement often throughout this book, "God does not call extraordinary people; He calls ordinary people who have chosen to pursue Him with their whole heart."

A word of caution: Do not make the mistake of comparing your walk with God with that of anyone else. There are people who have walked with God for many years. They may seem to know Him much more intimately than you do, but do not be discouraged. As human relationships take time to grow, so it is with your relationship with God. On the other hand, there are people who have been in church for fifty years, yet they do not know any more about the Father than they did when they first got saved. Time alone does not result in depth of relationship. God calls us and woos us, but we determine how deeply our relationship with Him will develop. The level of our hunger and the intensity of our pursuit determine the depth of that relationship. Some may say, "Jesse, I really desire God, but what can I do? How do I begin or where do I begin?" It begins with a longing and desire for Him that is lived out every day in our prayer life and personal devotions.

Sometimes people think prayer is getting on their knees and rattling off a long list of wants and needs, but it is more than that. It is talking to the Father in the same manner as you would talk to your friend or spouse or loved one. You pour out your heart, not worrying about being politically correct or saying a lot of religious words like "thee" and "thou." In other words, you just be yourself and share your heart with Him. What is awesome is that even though God knows your dreams and desires, He wants you to share them with Him anyway. Besides prayer, there are what I call disciplines that you can add to your life to strengthen your walk with Him, such as fasting, which helps to quiet the flesh and awaken the spirit part of us. And going to church regularly where we find strength and fellowship of others of like-mindedness. This is why I say drawing close to Him will cost us something. The Father longs so much for our fellowship and intimate friendship, He will want more and more time alone with just you. He is willing; are you? He desires that we draw as close as possible; do you desire the same?

God is grieved when a person tastes of salvation and stops there. In Hebrews 6:1, the apostle Paul says that it is time to move beyond basic doctrine to the meatier things of the

Word. In 1 Corinthians 3:1, Paul calls those in the church "babes"! Just because a person lays hands on someone and that person falls down or because a minister can preach or teach well, doesn't prove the quality of their walk with God. It is not difficult to open the Bible and pull out a good sermon. There are many books available to help develop sermons, but I am not satisfied with that. I want to know what is on God's heart. When a person has spent time alone with God, in prayer and reading His Word, and they open up the Word to teach or preach, their words become alive with power and fire that is life-changing for the hearer!

Notice what the people said when they heard Christ speak, "He taught them as one having authority, and not as the scribes" (Matt. 7:29). When the disciples were arrested for preaching about Christ, the religious rulers were amazed at these unlearned men who had been with Jesus (Acts 4:13). This does not mean that we should not go to college, if given the chance, or that we should not study good books. I have done both, but Bible college only taught me facts about God. My hunger for God and pursuit of relationship with Him led me to Him.

During the Last Supper, Christ looked at His disciples and said, "From henceforth, I call you not servants; for the servant knoweth not what his lord doeth, but I have called you friends; for all things that I have heard of my Father I have made known unto you" (John 15:15). Did you grasp the significance of what Christ said? Servants do not know what their lord is doing, but friends do! God longs to share what is on His heart, but only His friends are eligible to hear. Notice that Jesus was not speaking to everyone, but to His disciples. Does that mean that only a chosen few are His friends? No, it does not. But just as we do not share personal things with all our friends, neither does Christ. I have many friends in the church and in the ministry, but very, very few are considered my close personal friends. There are fewer still in whom I confide. And none of my closest confidants are as close to me as my wife. She is by far my best friend, and the level of intimacy we share is only between us.

How God longs to bring us close to His heart where we truly are His intimate friends. Concerning the degree of intimacy in a relationship or friendship, consider the twelve disciples of Christ. Within that small group, it seems that three were closer to Him than the others: Peter, James, and John. They were with Him on the Mount of Transfiguration and at other notable times in the life of Jesus. Then among those three, John, who would lay his head on Christ while they sat around the table eating and fellowshiping, enjoyed an even closer relationship with the Master. It was John who, banished on the Isle of Patmos in his nineties, would be given the final revelation to the church in the book of Revelation. God does reveal His heart to those who walk close to Him.

One way I explain intimacy with God is by describing it as a move from the living room to the bedroom, from outside the secret place to inside the secret place. Abraham heard God's voice and—either because he had heard of His acts with Noah and Enoch or because he just had a burning desire in his heart—he said, "I want more!" Thus began an incredible journey that would culminate in God's description: "Abraham was My friend."

The secret place that I am referring to is the place where it is only you and the Father in the realm of the Spirit. Though in the physical it could be your front room or closet, or even your car, when once you block out all the distractions of the world and your surroundings, it is only you two. And in the spirit realm, you and the Father are alone, communing quietly. I have found this place many times, even while driving down the road, but to really be alone with Him, I can't be worried about traffic or the kids or what is on television, so I'll find a place of quietness and focus my thoughts and attention only on Him. Psalms 91:1 says, "He that dwelleth in the secret place of the Most High shall abide under the shadow of the Almighty." The secret place is that place of intimate communion with the Father. I usually begin my time alone with the Father with a love song; there are so many to sing to Him. I find this usually helps to clear my mind and focus it on Him. During this most intimate time, I may begin to weep as I sit in His presence adoring Him, loving Him, desiring to be close enough to Him to touch Him and hold Him close. Can't you feel the Father tugging at your heart? Sometimes I will get so caught up in worship that I will forget my needs and wants and just lay before Him adoring Him and completely lost in His presence. Talking about it makes me want to even now go join Him in sweet communion and fellowship. Why don't you lay this book down for a few minutes and meet with the Father. He is always waiting for us to come and spend time alone with Him.

It is difficult to fathom the magnitude of being called a friend of God. God Almighty, the Creator of the universe, wants to become my friend. We get excited when a famous sports figure signs his or her autograph. We are excited, too, when a well-known minister comes to town—especially if he or she prays for us personally. Yet Someone far greater wants us to know Him intimately, and He places His signature on our hearts. With His signature also comes something more valuable: Time spent with Him—not just in passing, as you would speak to someone on the street. If you so desire, you can have real, meaningful, communion with God. He has the ability to give Himself completely to all those with whom He walks. While I am in Florida worshiping God, you can be on the other side of the world worshiping Him and have His undivided attention at the same time. No human can give you that—only our awesome, incredible God!

Abraham not only built altars in worship, he also followed God's directives. This obedience represents another key to walking with Him. I pray often, "Holy Spirit, develop in me a hearing ear and an obedient heart." So, like Abraham, I not only hear Him speaking to my spirit, but I am also obedient to Him.

A very interesting event that happened in Abraham's life was the appearance of the pre-incarnate Christ. (See Genesis

18.) Pre-incarnate is a word that refers to a bodily appearance of Christ prior to His being born in the flesh. In Genesis 18, we find Him not only talking to Abraham but also having lunch with him. This took place after many years had passed since God commanded Abraham to leave his family. During that time, Abraham communed often with God and was obedient in everything God required.

One of his greatest tests of love and obedience came when God asked Abraham to offer his son, Isaac, as a sacrifice. (See Genesis 22.) As with Abraham, the closer we get to God, the more He will require of us. Just as Israel was held to a higher standard than the heathen nations, so are we—and even more so when God draws us close and shares His heart. When God asked for Abraham's son, He was testing Abraham's love for Him over his love for his son of promise. God wanted to know if He held Abraham's entire heart or only part of it. Often as Christians we give God only a small part of our heart when He desires all of it. As you may know, Abraham passed the test; His obedience was more far reaching than just that spot on the mountain. It reaches even to you and me today, for we are told, "So then they which be of faith are blessed with faithful Abraham" (Gal. 3:9).

We should not question the Father's commands even if we do not know the outcome of our obedience. His proving of Abraham is similar to one spouse asking the other, "Do you love me?" God asks that question often by commanding us to do something, or to go somewhere, or to say something. Samuel said to King Saul one day, "Behold, to obey is better than sacrifice" (1 Sam. 15:22). It was through sacrifices that men atoned for their sins and worshiped God. To say obedience to the Father was greater even than sacrifice places ultimate value on obedience.

God was so moved by this man, Abraham, that He named paradise after him! Up to the time of Christ, when a saint died, they did not go to heaven, as we know heaven to be; they went to a place called "paradise." Luke 16 tells us of a rich man and a beggar named Lazarus who died. The rich man was tormented in Hades, while Lazarus was carried into "Abraham's bosom" (v. 22). Referring to paradise as "Abraham's bosom" to me speaks volumes about the type of relationship God had with Abraham. Even today, when we want to honor a person for their life's work or to create a legacy for them, we do so by naming something after them. Some churches put the name of the person who provided the funds on the building. Some of our ships in the U. S. Navy are named after presidents or great generals. I believe God was honoring His friend by referring to paradise as "Abraham's bosom."

Earlier, I mentioned that Christ came to Abraham's place to eat lunch. Christ was on His way to destroy Sodom and stopped by to tell Abraham about it. He said, "Shall I hide from Abraham that thing which I do?" (Gen. 18:17). What an incredible thought! The Father honored their friendship by letting Abraham know His plans. The Bible says, "Surely the LORD GOD will do nothing, but he revealeth his secret unto his servants the prophets" (Amos 3:7). This is true not only in the sense of His dealings with the church, but also His involvement in the affairs of people. To be in a position where God shares His heart requires that we, like Abraham, lay down everything and give Him one hundred percent of our heart. He will test our hearts, lest it be said of us as it was of Israel, "Wherefore the Lord said, Forasmuch as this people draw near me with their mouth, and with their lips do honour me, but have removed their heart far from me..." (Isa. 29:13). God sees our innermost desires and motives and knows if our hearts are sincere.

As you look at Abraham, you see that he desired nothing from God other than a relationship with Him. Though in the physical realm Abraham did desire a son, He showed His love and trust to the Father by being willing to give Isaac, his son, back to Him in Genesis 22. Jesus said, "Seek ye first the kingdom of God and His righteousness, and all these things shall be added unto you" (Matt. 6:33). God wants us to want Him more than we want His blessings. Abraham showed that when he was willing to offer his son Isaac to

God. Similarly you do not choose friends for the mere sake of trying to get something from them. Relationships meet needs that are part of our makeup as humans. We all need friendship, emotional support and companionship, but we should not choose friends with the purpose of trying to extract from them something to satisfy our selfish desires. The desire for companionship and fellowship is not selfish. The desire to obtain position or things by our association or relationship with someone is selfish.

In seeking relationship with God, we need to seek Him not for His blessings, though they will come; nor for His gifts, though they will come as well. We should seek Him for Himself! Abraham did not follow after God for His blessings; he followed Him because he longed to know Him. Out of that relationship, God entrusted His blessings to him.

Another benefit of intimate friendship with God is that He will allow our prayers to change His mind or plan of action. When the Lord revealed to Abraham the judgment about to fall on Sodom and Gomorrah, Abraham said, "Wilt thou also destroy the righteous with the wicked?" (Gen. 18:23). The Lord eventually said if He could find ten righteous, He would not destroy Sodom and Gomorrah. Had Abraham not stopped at ten, what number would have withheld the judgment of God? I believe that had Abraham not stopped at ten, God would have spared Sodom, all for the sake of one man who was His friend. The time will come when we are living with Him in heaven that we will probably meet those who prayed for us and spoke to God on our behalf. As we will discuss later, Moses' intercession also stayed the hand of God against the rebellious, complaining Israelites.

It is incredible that a mere human could touch God's heart as Abraham did. It reminds me of Queen Esther in the book that bears her name. Esther went before the king, although she had not been summoned. In doing so she put her life in jeopardy. Because of the king's love for her, he beckoned her to come near and to share her heart with him. As she did, she became an instrument of God to save her entire nation.

God longs for us to draw near to Him and to share our hearts with Him. Although He knows our every need; as a loving Father, He wants to hear us pour out our hearts to Him. The Bible shows us that Abraham was not a perfect man. This should encourage and comfort us. It shows us that no matter how close we get to God, we are not immune from failure or mistakes. As long as we live in this flesh, we will have to deal with our shortcomings and our sin nature. The good news, though, is that the closer we draw to God, the easier it is for us to live victoriously over the flesh. As we draw close to Him through spending time with Him in prayer and in the reading of His Word, we absorb more of His nature and His mindset. As our love for God grows, so does our hatred for sin. In time we develop a loathing for sin, discovering that deliberate sin literally makes us sick just thinking about it. Our sensitivity to things that grieve God will increase to such a point that the Holy Spirit can immediately get our attention if we are about to grieve Him.

As I look at today's church as a whole and meet Christians every day, I see more and more compromise with the world in their lives. There are many who are fearful, depressed, or anxious about the future. Entering God's presence will change these oppressive conditions. Many ministers say, "Come to church and allow God to remove your burdens." Yet many who come to church to have their burdens removed, end up walking out still carrying those same heavy burdens. The reason for this may be in part because we are not experiencing the concentrated manifest presence of God in many of our churches. The question that is often asked is, "Does God still manifest His presence in power?" Emphatically, the answer is yes. The scripture is still true, "Jesus Christ, the same yesterday, today and for ever" (Heb. 13:8). As we will discuss in the next chapter, throughout the Old and New Testaments, God showed up on the scene in such a way that people could tangibly feel and visibly see Him. If He did it then, He will do it again when our hunger for Him exceeds all our other desires.

Abraham put God first in his life. For that reason, he enjoyed a powerful and intimate relationship with God. Reading about Abraham makes me hungry for that kind of relationship. I do not want my friendship with God just to be a casual acquaintance. I want it to rival the friendship that Abraham had with Him. I want it to be a close intimate friendship, even more real than I have had with people. I can hear God whispering, "Come closer; draw nearer still; I long for intimate communion and friendship with you. As I walked with Adam, Enoch and Abraham, and shared many things with them, so I long to walk with you."

Can you hear Him? Do you sense His nearness? The Father always draws near to those who desire to walk with Him. What will your answer be when He calls for you to separate yourself from the familiar and step out into what He has especially for you? I know what I will say to Him: "Okay, Father, here I am. I am coming after You with everything that lies within me!"

*"Moses went into
the midst of the cloud…"*

—*EXODUS* 24:18

CHAPTER 5

MOSES

Into His Presence,
Part I

One of Moses' first dramatic encounters with God took place in the desert while he was alone tending his father-in-law's flock. It was there that Moses caught a glimpse of the burning bush. As he drew near this marvelous sight, he was fascinated with the fire that burned within the bush, yet did not consume the bush. It was the fire of God's presence. It was not the bush not being burned or consumed that drew Moses closer, it was the fire. As Moses drew near, the Lord spoke and said, "Take off your shoes, for the ground you stand on is holy" (Exod. 3:5, author's paraphrase).

Not long ago the Holy Spirit said to me, "The reason Moses had to remove his shoes was because once you enter My presence, you can no longer stand upon, or depend upon, your own strength and ways." In His presence it is all about Him. God wants our lives to become like the burning bush; He wants the fire of His presence to burn within us so that others are drawn to His presence in our lives. We become as burning bushes when people are not impressed with our words; they are drawn to the fire of His presence when it is God speaking through us.

From this supernatural encounter, Moses began walking with God in a dimension that he had not previously known. I am certain that during the forty years Moses spent in the desert he communed with God, or contemplated the things he knew about Him. Remember, although he was raised in Pharaoh's household, his natural mother, Jochebed, cared for him for the first few years of his life. (See Exodus 2.) You can be certain that Jochebed told her precious son as much as she could about the Most High God of Israel. Yet, Moses seemed destined to an ordinary life of exile, tending flocks in the desert. God uses the deserts—the lonely places of our lives—to direct our thoughts and our hearts to Him. And on this day in that forsaken desert, Moses met God personally in an encounter that not only delivered him from that desert, but forever changed His life.

Some encounters or experiences with the Father leave a deeper impression on us than others. Some so affect us that we come back to Him for more. No doubt after his burning bush experience, something was birthed in Moses that he could not stop thinking about. God had spoken to him! And who was he that God would speak to him? Surely, he was no prophet, and he was definitely no saint. He had committed murder some forty years earlier. He was not living on the back side of the desert because he enjoyed the solitude. No, he was still in hiding, for he knew if Pharaoh ever got his hands on him that he would die for his crime. But any fears that Moses may have had about his past slowly began to fade after God spoke with him.

We can only imagine what was going through Moses' mind as God spoke with him about his destiny and calling. We know that after the Lord told him that he was going to be sent back to Egypt as God's spokesperson, Moses used one excuse after another trying to change God's mind. Like Moses, there are times when we may feel inadequate for the calling on our lives. Whether it is working in the nursery at church, working in bus ministry or even preaching behind a pulpit, you may look at your present situation and think, "No way God; not me!" Moses tried that; he even told God that he could not speak eloquently. (See Exodus 4:10–11.) As a young man, Moses would have been trained in the finest schools of Egypt. He should have been a great speaker; however, forty years on the back side of a desert can break even the strongest person. Therefore, when God called, Moses was certain that God had dialed the wrong number.

It amazes me the number of Christians who feel the same way. Usually it is the life on the back side of a lonely desert that brings a person to that point. Rather than seeing the potential in themselves that God sees, they do not pursue Him. "Why should I?" they argue. "Surely God is not interested in someone with a past, or someone with issues, right?" Wrong! And again I say wrong! God views us from the perspective of our completed end, not our incomplete beginning. When God looked at Moses walking in the desert, possibly thinking about his lonely life or the things he might have accomplished had he not messed up in Egypt, God looked down and said, "There is a man I can use." Thankfully, God sees potential in us when we or others do not.

After Moses' failed attempt at talking God into finding someone else, he reluctantly accepted God's calling, though God did allow him to use Aaron as his mouthpiece. What is so amazing about this encounter with God is that His presence can bring an end to years of heartache and loneliness. What was true for Moses is true for us. One moment in God's presence can, and will, change any situation and undo the years of pain and loneliness. There is so much to learn from Moses' life. He experienced God in a way that few have experienced; Moses experienced God's awesome glory.

Look forward to the exodus. (See Exodus 12–14.) As Moses was leading the children of Israel out of Egypt, they reached the Red Sea. God made His presence known in a cloud by day and a pillar of fire by night, shielding the

Israelites from the Egyptian army. (See Exodus 14:19.) God's presence will always set us apart from others. Many false religions claim that the power or presence of God is with them, but it is nothing more than a demonic illusion. Unfortunately, many of the modern-day churches have not been able to boast about having the presence of God with them either. We are able to come up with catchy names for our churches and power-sounding slogans, but when people show up, all they find are shallow sermons and hyped-up musicians. We have become experts at teaching people about God and giving history lessons, but where are the modern-day examples?

Thank God there are some churches that have moved beyond history lessons and into His presence. As I have said before, whenever I mention His presence, I am not talking about His omnipresence, which is God everywhere, but about His concentrated, manifest presence. That is what many of our churches lack today. Is it any wonder that people come searching for Him and leave disappointed? They have heard the slogans and catchy phrases; they have seen the power sounding, eye-catching signs, but when they showed up, there was no visible or tangible sign of God. Pentecostals and charismatic churches have been singing and praising God for many years. We have had some awesome services; people have been healed; people have been delivered and saved. There have been some great sermons preached. Unfortunately, we have stopped there, and rather than pushing on into the deeper things of God we have stopped waist deep in the river of His presence. (See Ezekiel 47.) We have stopped at the foot of the mountain, rather than going to the top where God has camped out waiting for us to climb up and commune with Him. As you have already read and learned, it is God's will for us to go deeper in Him. He does not want us to get to a comfortable place and stop. That is how Israel failed to conquer the whole Promised Land; they took much of the land of Canaan, then settled down. Despite the fact that the Lord said that there was still much land to be taken, they stopped and did not go any further and capture the lands promised to them. (See Joshua 13:1.)

When you look at what God did in the Old and New Testaments, you can see that we fall short of our capacity for relationship with Him. I praise God that people are getting saved, but knowing there is more, I want more! In the book of Acts we read that when the shadow of Peter touched people, they were healed immediately. (See Acts 5:15.) When has that happened since? What God intends as the norm for us, is actually the exception. Perhaps the reason we cannot look at a crippled person today and say, as Peter did in Acts 3:6, "Such as I have give I thee: In the name of Jesus Christ of Nazareth, rise up and walk," is because all we have are history lessons of what God once did. But God does not change! He is not any less present now than He was then. The problem is the level of our intensity in our desire for His presence.

The early church lived for one thing and only one thing—that was for Christ and His gospel. The history of the early church, as seen in the book of Acts, shows that the believers were totally devoted to spreading the good news of Jesus Christ. Radical? Yes, but they were still in their right minds, even though their thoughts were consumed with Him. John said in the book of Revelation that those who overcame the enemy did not love their own lives. (See Revelation 12:11.) In other words, this life was not of great importance to them; they were not caught up with their own selfish pursuits. Perhaps the reason we do not see God breaking out in our churches and over our cities is because we love our own lives more than we love Him. This devotion to God may be difficult to comprehend. Sadly, the evidence against the church is mounting; we would rather save face with the world than to seek His face.

Some may say, "It may be true that we do not experience His presence like Moses did, but God is still using us." You know what? They are right. God is using us; people are getting saved; people are getting healed. However, that does not mean that God does not want us to draw yet closer. Think of how much more we could accomplish for Him if we knew His heartbeat. Think of how much more we could accomplish if we stepped out of the way and let Him flow through us the way He longs to do. There would be no room for showmanship or pride as we press deeper into His presence.

Because of His mercy, He will use what He can; just ask Balaam! (See Numbers 22:5–33.) Even though God spoke through Balaam's donkey, we will not find that little donkey in heaven. I can speak prophetically that God's heart is broken because much of His bride is living apart from dependence on Him. We think that we know what is best. We think that we can do His work with our catchy slogans and well-planned methods. We think that we only need Him when we preach. Not so. God wants to run the whole show from start to finish! When will we step out of the way and just become a vessel He can use? While it is true that God is moving in some places, the church could be much more powerful and effective. I just want the church to realize that God longs for deeper intimacy with His bride. My wife would still remain with me even if our intimate moments were few and far between the normal activities of marriage, but she would long for more from me. God also longs for more from His bride! If He is so willing, why aren't we? As we will see in Moses' life, the answer to that question may very well be that we are not willing to pay the price to go deeper.

I am hungry for more of God, and I will not be satisfied until I am so full of Him that when I step outside in the morning, my shadow heals someone! I will not be satisfied until God so engulfs our churches with the supernatural fire of the burning bush that people who come in will sense they need to remove their shoes because the very ground they stand on is holy. I will not be satisfied until the tangible, manifest presence of God breaks forth in our midst. And you know what? My prayer for our church and the body of Christ is this, "O God, may our hunger for You be such that the heavens are opened, and Your concentrated manifest presence falls on this place!"

I thank the Lord that there are a growing number of hungry people being raised up who want nothing but Him. These people come to church not to be entertained, but to enter into the presence of God. They do not seek to draw attention to themselves, but rather seek to be drawn to Him. Hungry people are not impressed with how well the preacher can articulate a message or move the crowd. Hungry people only want to know if God is there because they only want Him. When preachers get alone with God, they will preach with more power and minister more effectively. When Christians get alone with God, their walk with God becomes stronger, and they become better witnesses for Christ. Both preachers and laypeople will become true followers of Christ.

The anointing enables us to accomplish for God what we are each called to do. When we find that place where He is, we are changed! When we emerge from His presence, people know that He is near when we speak. It is possible to get so close to Him that others can sense His presence everywhere we go. There is a difference between the anointing for service and His manifest presence. The purpose of the anointing is to destroy every yoke (Isa. 10:27); therefore, we are anointed for service. This divine anointing enables us to fulfill the tasks we are called to do. Otherwise, we could not accomplish anything eternal. However, the manifest presence of God involves drawing near to Him in intimate friendship. The anointing is about us and our empowering for what we are doing and saying for Him. The manifest presence of God is about Him and what He is doing and saying to us and through us.

The anointing can be abused, as we see in the life of Samson (see Judges 14–16) and in Saul, Israel's first king who failed miserably. But God's manifest presence cannot be abused nor manipulated. We have all seen ministers strut across the platform trying to impress the crowd with their antics. They draw attention to themselves as if they were the church's version of a Hollywood movie star. Yet when God shows up, there is no strutting, no pride, no stroking of the ego, no attempting to impress the crowd.

From my own experience, I know it feels good to stand behind the pulpit when the words I am speaking are flowing under an anointing faster than I can comprehend. It feels good to finish a message and have people come around, stroking your ego by telling you it was the best message they have ever heard. It feels good to walk into a room of ministers and be acknowledged as a servant of God. But did God receive any glory? Perhaps I impressed people, but the real question is, "Did I impress Him?" People may have said that I preached great, but what did God say? For a long time I was caught up in the praise of people, but no more! No longer do I care whether people are impressed with me. No longer do I preach messages hoping to impress people or stir up their emotions. All I care about is whether I get God's attention. Now, more than ever, I am only concerned with leading people into His presence.

Paul the Apostle wrote to the Corinthian church, "As we behold the glory of the Lord, we are changed into the same image, from glory to glory" (2 Cor. 3:18, author's paraphrase). The cure for those who have problems with secret sin is to get them into God's presence so He can touch them. His presence also cures pride. It is hard, if not impossible, to be prideful when you are in His presence. In His presence you realize that you are nothing outside of Him. Are you hungry for His presence yet?

As the children of Israel stood before the Red Sea, the cloud of His presence was behind them. This miraculous cloud was not only visible to them, but also to the Egyptians. As you draw closer to the Lord and become more like Him in your character, non-Christians will be drawn to you. People at work who once would have nothing to do with you will suddenly be drawn to you. They will come asking questions about God or seeking advice on some issue. They will come to you for prayer needs. On the other hand, you might be standing in line at the grocery store and people will become agitated with you for no apparent reason. Their agitation will be because the enemy at work in them can see God's hand on you. It is amazing that those who are hurting will be drawn to us, and those who are under the enemy's control will be agitated with us! It is reported that as Charles Finney, a well-known evangelist in the 1800s, walked through a mill one day, some of the workers were so overcome with conviction they started falling on the floor, weeping and asking for God's mercy! That is an example of living in the presence of God.

What I am talking about is not new. God has always had people whose hunger for Him exceeded all other desires. Because of the intensity of their hunger, they have had a personal encounter with Him. Unfortunately, these people are in the minority when compared to those who are satisfied with their walk with God. Naturally, we cannot say that God loves them any less or that God will not use them. God does love them and He does use them. But He longs to draw them closer to Himself than is possible, considering the casual walk they have accepted. I do not want to get to heaven and find out that, because I was satisfied with my walk and level of intimacy, I did not accomplish everything I could have. Neither do I want to get to heaven and find that I fell far short of becoming the man of God I could have become had I given myself over more fully to God. Do you? That is the whole issue!

Are you satisfied with your level of intimacy? The life of Moses teaches us something about that. After crossing the Red Sea, the Israelites journeyed to Mount Sinai. It was here that the Lord commanded Moses to separate the people and to prepare them for a holy visitation. If we are ever going to see God break out in our churches and experience an open heaven over our lives and cities, we must prepare ourselves to go into the presence of God. God only shows up when people have hungered after Him and have prepared themselves, and thus have made a place for Him. Every person to whom God spoke in the Bible and who responded to His call, experienced more of Him. The Father draws and woos us, but He will never force himself upon anyone. Each person can choose to accept or to reject Him. When He calls a person, His desire is for them to accept His invitation and for the pursuit to begin; however, if that person does not respond, He moves on—even though it grieves His heart.

It was at Mount Sinai that God told Moses "And thou shalt set bounds unto the people round about, saying, Take heed to yourselves, that ye go not up into the mount, or touch the border of it" (Exod. 19:12). This warning was issued not because God did not want them to experience His manifest presence, but because He knew that they were not yet prepared for that level of relationship. Remember, there are levels of friendship with God. Moses was at a different level than others. Later, when the opportunity came for them to experience more of Him, the people declined: "And they said unto Moses, Speak thou with us, and we will hear: but let not God speak with us, lest we die" (Exod. 20:19). They were telling Moses, "You go, Moses; we are afraid to get that close to God. We do not want to get that close to God." How sad; but many today do the same thing. Many people have changed churches because the intensity of the worship became too great, or the price of discipleship was too high. It became easier for them to leave rather than to press onward into God's presence.

A similar situation existed in the New Testament church at Corinth. Listen to what Paul tells the Corinthians: "And I, brethren, could not speak unto you as unto spiritual, but as unto carnal, even as unto babes in Christ. I have fed you with milk, and not with meat: for hitherto ye were not able to bear it, neither yet now are ye able" (1 Cor. 3:1–2). Paul wanted to share the deeper things of faith with them, but he was unable to do so because their maturity level would not permit it. When Jesus made a bold statement about drinking His blood and eating His flesh (John 6:56), some of His followers said to Him, "This is too much; we are out of here." God's presence, or revealing of Himself, has more to do with the level of hunger in a person than their maturity level. Again, as in any relationship, there are levels of intimacy and friendship. Relationships deepen with time, but even more so with the level of hunger. The more you want, the more you get; the more you get, the more you want. You are never satisfied. You always want more of Him.

As Israel waited at the foot of Mount Sinai, they could see God's presence on the mountaintop. The dark clouds, the thunder and the lightning proclaimed His presence. At God's command, Moses began his walk up the mountain into His presence. Can you imagine what was going through his mind? All the other times God spoke, it had been in an audible voice, yet the voice was peaceful. Now, God's manifest presence had descended upon the mountain. No longer was there just the quiet voice of God. The very elements of nature thundered His presence. The book of Exodus gives us a vivid description:

> And it came to pass on the third day in the morning, that there were thunders and lightnings, and a thick cloud upon the mount, and the voice of the trumpet exceeding loud; so that all the people that was in the camp trembled. And mount Sinai was altogether on a smoke, because the LORD descended upon it in fire: and the smoke thereof ascended as the smoke of a furnace, and the whole mount quaked greatly.
>
> —Exodus 19:16, 18

Moses then heard the voice of God call him up the mountain. I am waiting, rather impatiently, for God to show up in such a demonstration of power that those who drive by our churches will slow down as they sense God's manifest presence. As Moses entered the dark clouds and came before His presence, God revealed to Moses His laws and commandments. After Moses had received the law, he went back to the people and had them pledge their obedience to God's Word.

This was also one of the saddest moments in Israel's history. It was while Moses was on the mountain in God's presence that the Israelites were at the base of the mountain worshiping the golden calf that they had made for an idol.

They were partying and dancing naked. Moses was then summoned back up the mountain where he spent the next forty days in God's presence. It was during this time of fasting and fellowship that God gave Moses the blueprint for the tabernacle and the ark of the covenant. The tabernacle and the ark were to be symbols of God's abiding presence.

This sad event tells us a couple of things about the presence of God. First, His manifest presence was visible on the mount. Second, even though His presence was visible from below, it had no impact on those outside of His presence. It is apparent from this that the Father can limit His presence to an area. Only those within the area of His presence will be impacted; those outside His presence will not be affected. For example, when Solomon dedicated the temple he had built for the Father, we are told the presence of God filled it, "So that the priests could not stand to minister because of the cloud: for the glory of the LORD had filled the house of the LORD" (1 Kings 8:11). No one outside the temple was affected, only those who were in the temple. It is not that people can resist His presence; no one can do that. It is rather that only those in the vicinity of His presence are affected. I have seen people resist the drawing of the Holy Spirit, but the Word makes it clear that when people step into His manifest presence, they cannot resist Him. People may be able to resist His wooing, but when His manifest presence invades a church or an area, no one, sinner or saint, can resist His presence. Some may ask, "If no one can resist His manifest presence, why does He not just show up, so everyone would repent and get saved?" God will not violate our free will. God wants our surrender to be voluntary and done out of a willing heart. He does not show up where He is not invited unless, of course, in His sovereignty He finds it necessary.

God is ever near and ready to intervene on our behalf, but that presence is different from His manifest presence. God was there with the Israelites in His omnipresence, but when He concentrated His manifest presence, only Moses was allowed to enter. It was the Lord who told Moses, "The people have defiled themselves; go back down from here" (Exod. 32:7). God was well aware of the people's actions, though they were not on the mountain. Because God is omnipresent, everywhere at all times, He is well aware of what we are facing and going through. We can find comfort in knowing that what Paul said is true for every child of God: That He will never leave us nor forsake us. (See Hebrews 13:5.) But I want more than His omnipresence. Just as when I am away from my family, my children know that my heart and thoughts are with them, yet nothing substitutes for my actually being there, holding them and loving on them. While I know that God is always near and that I am always in His thoughts, I want His manifest presence in my home and in my church. I want to touch Him and to feel His heartbeat!

There is a hunger for the presence of God sweeping the land. There is a growing number of God's people who want to see the Father's manifest presence inhabit His church. When our hunger exceeds all our other desires, He will answer us, and the church will be what God intended for His bride to be. The day is coming when satisfied saints and unconcerned sinners will not be able to just sit there while the Spirit blows upon us. It is so disheartening to see these disinterested people sit unmoved and unrepentant while the Holy Spirit is moving mightily upon a service. Some members of the congregation who are sensitive to the Holy Spirit will be crying; others will be dancing; the minister will be pleading for sinners to get saved. In the midst of all this, there will be those who do not care what God is doing; they are unmoved. Because the Holy Spirit is a Gentleman, He will bypass those who choose not to drink from the river of His presence as it flows. But one day, Father God will concentrate His presence over a church. When He passes over that place, the scene will look much like what you would have seen had you been with Isaiah, the prophet, when He caught a glimpse of the Father: "Then said I, Woe is me! for I am undone;

because I am a man of unclean lips, and I dwell in the midst of a people of unclean lips: for mine eyes have seen the King, the LORD of hosts" (Isa. 6:5). Isaiah appeared to be a righteous man by our standards, but when he saw the Father, all he could do was fall on his face and repent!

A couple of years ago while I was pastoring in Dade City, Florida, we were having an incredible time of worship when suddenly the atmosphere changed. I could sense that God was near. It was as if we were standing right outside the throne room. My wife, who was leading the worship, crumpled to the floor weeping. Our youth pastor's wife, who was on the platform with my wife, also fell to the floor weeping. While my brother-in-law was playing the keyboard for us, he began to cry as he tried to continue playing and singing. I began to shake uncontrollably; my breath was coming in short gasps. People behind me and around the church were crying; some were shrieking; someone was moaning. This invasion of God's presence was an answer to my prayers! Over and over I had prayed for Him to show up and take over our service. Yet there I was, standing in the middle of it, crying, barely able to breathe, begging God not to come any further! I remember crying, "No, Lord! Not yet, they will die!"

After the service I kept thinking, I have asked for Him, even begged Him to show up, and when He does, I ask Him to leave. I had not expected God to respond to our hunger for Him so quickly. When our hunger exceeded our desire for anything else, He showed up. We just did not know what to do once He came. As I look back now with sadness, I realize that we were unprepared for His glorious presence. That night in Dade City, there was no cloud, no lightning, just a touch of His manifest presence. I compare that moment to when Jesus was in the Garden of Gethsemane and the soldiers came to arrest Him. When the soldiers said they were looking for Jesus, His reply, "I am," caused them to fall backward. (See John 18:6.) At that moment, deity met flesh, and flesh had to bow. There is no evidence of anything extraordinary happening at that time—no lightning or thick clouds or fire—just the words of Jesus, speaking as God. His manifest presence is not always visible, but it is tangible and is always felt.

The Israelites felt comforted by the presence of God going before them as a pillar of fire by night and as a cloud by day. They enjoyed the safety of His feeding and "burping them." They welcomed His protection as He wiped out their enemies. Oh, but when He concentrated His presence on Mount Sinai and told them to separate and prepare themselves, and come near, they were wary. (See Exodus 19:10; 20:18.) Suddenly they were faced with a choice. The God who led them out of Egypt and watched over them was requiring more. God told Moses, "I want to make you a kingdom of priests" (Exod. 19:6). What did the Israelites do? They did the same thing we do so often when the Lord says to us, in effect, "I have enjoyed the dance and song, but now I want you to come nearer." They backed up. The Israelites told Moses, "You speak to God because if we do, we will die." (See Exodus 20:19.) There was truth in their words. They feared they would die physically. However, what really would have happened in His presence would have been the death of their fleshly desires and a cleansing consecration unto God, resulting in relationship with Him.

Moses went up the mountain to do what the others were afraid to do. I am determined that no one else will go for me; I want to go to God myself. I do not know what God would think or how He would feel, but if my children sent someone else in their place to speak to me, I would be disappointed and hurt. If they chose to stay outside rather than come into the house to enjoy my company, I would be hurt. Yet, we do the same thing to God. We get just so close to Him, then hesitate and stop. The Father is saying, "Why did you stop? Come nearer."

Intimacy with the Father is an awesome experience. Many churches have only been willing to walk down the aisle for the marriage and the party at the fellowship hall; they refuse to go to the honeymoon suite. The marriage is necessary in order to be joined with Christ, and the party of celebration is good as we enjoy the benefits of being married to Christ. Only those who move on to the honeymoon suite will enjoy the deeper intimacy of the marriage relationship. The Father longs for intimate friendship and communion, but some things just cannot be discovered while dancing and singing in the fellowship hall!

Getting alone with the Father and having precious communion with Him results in a closeness that is only found in the secret place. It is not the only place that you can build your relationship with the Father, but it is the only place where such close, intimate communion can be found. Jesus did not know the Father's heart because He hung out with the disciples, although fellowship with the disciples was good and needful. He knew the Father's heart because He would get away into the secret place and fellowship with Him, spending whole nights in prayer. What will sustain us in the time of need are not the moments we danced, shouted and sang in front of the veil, as good as that was. What will sustain us are the moments spent in the secret place. Dancing, shouting, and singing in His presence are wonderful, but they just do not compare or move us the same way as being in His presence in the secret place. I would rather just crawl up in His lap and feel His heartbeat than dance outside the door when He is near.

Are you hungry yet? Do you feel that longing in your heart that only He can satisfy? Tell Him that you are willing to go up the mount with Him into His presence. Tell Him that you want more than just a song and dance. Tell Him that you want to go to the secret place with Him. Tell Him that He is all you need and long for. We did not have a problem expressing our desires to our spouses when we dated them. We did not mind walking down the aisle with them. We did not mind going to the banquet hall with them to dance and party after the wedding. We definitely did not mind going to the honeymoon suite, to the secret place, to be intimately alone. So, why do we decline the Father's invitation when He says, "I want you to draw closer"?

The early church and a few individuals since that time have walked in a level of closeness with God that some today will never experience, simply because they do not choose to pursue Him. I refuse to be part of that sad majority! I refuse to enjoy less than what He intended for my relationship with Him to be! As we will see in the next chapter, there awaits a fellowship and communion with God, as seen in the life of Moses, which is available to all. Psalms 103:7 says "He made known His ways unto Moses, His acts unto the children of Israel." People outside the veil know about His acts, but only those in the secret place know His ways.

"Shew me thy glory..."

—Exodus 33:18

CHAPTER 6

MOSES

Into His Presence, Part II

Moses' hunger for God exceeded all other desires. (See Exodus 30.) Perhaps this intense hunger was birthed from the forty days on the mountain with God, or perhaps his intense hunger for communion with God began during the years of solitude in Midian, tending sheep. Perhaps it was a culmination of all these things that brought Moses to the place where he cried out, "Show me Your glory." People will always be brought to this point as they draw closer to God. The closer you draw to God, the closer you want to get to Him. Moses, like Enoch before him, could not get enough of fellowshiping with God. The closer Moses drew to God, the more desperate he became for a deeper, more intimate relationship with Him.

Exodus 33:11 says, "So the Lord spake to Moses face to face." When Aaron and Miriam spoke against Moses' authority, God said to them, "If there be a prophet among you, I the Lord will make myself known unto him in a vision, and will speak unto him in a dream. My servant Moses is not so, who is faithful in all mine house. With Him will I speak mouth to mouth" (Num. 12:6–8). What grips my attention in this amazing declaration is that God spoke to Moses "mouth to mouth," which we would call "face to face."

Earlier Aaron and Miriam had approached Moses saying, "Has the Lord indeed spoken only through Moses? Has he not spoken through us also?" (Num. 12:2). They had not only questioned Moses' authority, but his ability to hear from God as well. And, they were in fact, calling into question Moses' closeness with the Father.

In Exodus 33:20 God said, "You can't see My face; for no man shall see Me and live" (author's paraphrase). Yet in 33:11 we read that Moses spoke to God face to face, as a man does with his friend. This may seem to be a contradiction, but I asked the Lord why this was. His answer to me was, "Moses did not gaze upon My face. He was in My presence, and I spoke to him face to face. Just as a blind man knows that you are facing him because he can feel your breath, Moses felt My breath of life upon his face." If we could have glimpsed Moses speaking with God, perhaps we would have seen his hair softly moving as God spoke with him. It has been said that when God's presence filled the tabernacle as the priest sprinkled the blood on the ark of the covenant, the veil would begin to move, and there would be a whooshing sound as His presence filled the holy of holies. Again, the closer you get to God, the closer you want to get.

In Exodus 33:13, Moses stood in the completed tabernacle and said to God, "Show me Thy way that I might know You" (author's paraphrase). Psalms 103:7 tells us that God answered that prayer. The psalmist writes, "He made known His ways unto Moses, His acts unto the children of Israel." After months of walking with God, who was visibly present in the cloud and pillar of fire, after seeing His mighty miracles in Egypt, after spending forty days with Him alone on a mountain, Moses still prayed, "Show me Your glory!" Only a hungry person would say this after experiencing all that Moses had experienced.

Ezekiel 47 tells us of a river that flows from the throne of God. It begins ankle deep and eventually becomes a river to swim in. It is the river of His presence, and the closer to Him you draw, the deeper He will draw you. God's presence is unfathomable! He is beyond understanding! We will never get to a place in our spiritual walk where there is nothing more to discover or know about Him. Paul, the apostle who walked with God for many years and who received so much revelation insight, still prayed that he might "know" God. (See Philippians 3:10.) Paul's desire was to become even more intimately acquainted with Him. The word Paul used here for *know* was the word *genosko,* which means "to come to know, to become acquainted with; a Jewish idiom for sexual intercourse between a man and a woman." Paul experienced the same intense desire for a deeper relationship with God that Moses experienced. After walking with God and experiencing things that you and I long to experience, Moses was not satisfied, he could only cry out, "I want more of You, Father. I am not satisfied. I want to know You more." Where most people would have stopped, Moses pressed onward. That is the intensity level that you and I must desire and press into if we are to ever move beyond the veil into His presence.

God rewards hunger—not just a desire for knowledge, but a holy hunger for Him. When your desperation and hunger for Him exceeds your desire for anything or anyone else, you will meet Him! God's response to Moses was, "My presence will go with you, and I will give you rest" (Exod. 33:14, author's paraphrase). Notice Moses' bold reply, "If your presence goes not with us, carry us not up" (v. 15, author's paraphrase). I think that reply made the Father smile. Moses' reply, "We are not going anywhere without You!" showed that he recognized the importance of his relationship with the Father. As a leader, Moses recognized the importance of having God in control. Though the people were not always sold out in their pursuit of God, Moses was sold out to Him both as Israel's leader and in his own personal life.

In Exodus 33:16 Moses said, "For wherein shall it be known here that I and thy people have found grace in thy sight? Is it not in that thou goest with us? So shall we be separated, I and thy people, from all the people that are upon the face of the earth." That which would separate Israel from all other nations was God's presence. Moses said that not just Israel, but Moses also would be separated unto Him. This was God's intention from the very beginning, to separate the nation of Israel from other nations. God separated the nation of Israel by His very presence with them as they traveled through the wilderness. Sadly, many years later Israel would desire to be like the other nations and have a king rule over them rather than God.

In Exodus 33:17 we read God's reply to Moses' request for God's presence to go with them: "I will do this thing also that thou has spoken, for thou hast found grace in my sight, and I know thee by name." That is the kind of relationship I long to experience with the Father. Does God know each of us by name? Of course He does. As God, He knows us, but the word for *know* in the original Hebrew means to know personally and intimately. The Father is trying to teach us that there is a level of friendship and communion that can be obtained with Him and goes beyond the ordinary. Abraham was called His friend. Enoch went for a walk with Him and decided not to come home. Moses enjoyed deep communion with Him. God was saying, "Because of his passionate pursuit of Me, I do not just know Moses as an acquaintance, I know him as an intimate, personal friend."

Some people are caught up in making an impression on others when their concern should be to make an impression on God. He is the One who blesses us. It is He who either raises us up or brings us down. In other words, the motive behind our pursuit should be pure and should place God as primary importance. Jesus said, "Seek ye first the kingdom of God, and his righteousness" (Matt. 6:33). Moses did not care if he was well liked or popular. He was in pursuit of God and what God thought of him. As you study the life of

Moses, you will find him communing with God—so much so that Exodus 34:29 says, "When he came down from the mount…Moses knew not that the skin of his face shone while he talked with Him" (author's paraphrase). That glow never went away as he continued in communion and fellowship in the tabernacle. Such was the sight that the people were afraid of him. (See Exodus 34:30.) They asked that Moses keep a veil over his face to cover the effects of the glory of God upon him. What they were seeing was the effect of Moses spending time alone with God.

When a person begins spending time with the Father, the effects of such sweet communion will be evident. In the book of Acts we read that people were healed as the apostle Peter's shadow touched them. People were healed by handkerchiefs that the apostle Paul had prayed over. And in modern times, I have read accounts of people like Charles Finney and Smith Wigglesworth who had a profound impact on people, just walking by them on the street. These are examples of the results of a tangible touch of God's presence on the lives of those who have drawn close to Him. That is what I long to see again and to experience personally. I want to come from His presence with the residual effects of being in His presence still lingering upon me. God does not favor some people over others; these phenomena result from being in His presence.

This type of relationship with the Father that we have been reading about and longing for is not something to be taken lightly. It should not even be considered as a short-term experience. It is not a one-time touch, although many people treat it as such. Unfortunately, when we have an awesome move of God at church, and God may really leave a mark on us or use us in some special way, too often after the service, we go back to our lives as usual. Such holy visitations and heavenly touches are sent from God to do more than just minister to us or through us. They are His way of stirring our hunger up for Him. We usually leave those services saying, "Didn't we have a good time today? That was certainly a good sermon tonight! Didn't the pastor preach great today?" We put so much emphasis on ourselves that God is barely mentioned. What will He say to us when we finally meet Him in heaven? What will our response to Him be as to why we did not draw closer after being surrounded by so great a cloud of witnesses?

One reason God recorded the lives of people such as Moses and Enoch was so that we would catch their hunger and pursue the Father for ourselves. What amazes me is to hear Christians and ministers, alike, say, "I wish that I could be used of God like that," or "I wish that I could know Him like some of the people in the Bible did." With what we have in the Word and the enabling of the Holy Spirit, we should not feel that it is impossible to attain a closer walk with the Father, a walk which is equal to or exceeds that of those who went before us. The question is, "Just how hungry are you? What price are you willing to pay?" Moses had to leave his comfort zone and assume leadership for millions of people. With such an awesome responsibility placed upon him, Moses drew near to the Father. The level of his relationship with God was incredible.

We learned from Abraham that it is possible to change God's intentions (as in when Abraham negotiated with God concerning the destruction of Sodom). Numbers 14:19 shows us one of the many times Moses interceded on behalf of the children of Israel. Only a person with a close relationship with God could stand before Him and stop divine judgment from coming. I believe that when we stand before the Father in heaven, we will see people who stayed the hand of God over nations simply by their powerful prayers of intercession. The Father hearkened to them because of their relationship with Him.

As we continue to consider Moses' incredible relationship with God, we read about the following incident that occurred after the completion of the tabernacle: "Then the cloud covered the tabernacle of meeting, and the glory of the LORD filled the tabernacle. And Moses was not able to enter the tabernacle of meeting, because the cloud rested above it, and the glory of the LORD filled the tabernacle" (Exod. 40:34–35). The presence of God in the tabernacle was such that not even Moses was able to enter. I have heard people say that they have experienced such a heavy presence of God that they have had to ask Him to stop because they could not bear it any longer. The fact that Moses could not enter tells me something about the power of God's presence. God can either show up in such a demonstration of power that we cannot stand, or as He so often does, He can limit His presence so that we are able to still function in a somewhat orderly way.

Another important lesson to be learned from the life of Moses is that those who pursue Him must handle with reverence the things God reveals and the gifts He gives. Because of his disobedience to God's command, Moses was not allowed to enter the Promised Land. (See Numbers 20.) The people were thirsty and needed water. God had told Moses to command the rock, and water would come out. Because Moses was upset with the attitude of the people, he struck the rock instead of speaking to it. God graciously allowed the water to gush out. But because of his disobedience, Moses was not allowed to lead the people into the Promised Land. The Lord told Moses in verse 12, "Because ye believed me not, to sanctify me in the eyes of the children of Israel, therefore ye shall not bring this congregation into the land which I have given them."

Some might question the severity of this punishment. After all, Moses was so close to God; why did God not just let this mistake slide? The Lord spoke to me about the severity of His judgments one day when I was studying another passage. In 1 Samuel 6, we read about the Philistines taking the ark of the covenant, God's symbol of His abiding presence, from Israel during a battle. While the Philistines had the ark in their possession, they were plagued with God's judgment. Some people got very sick; others battled boils; some even died. Finally, the Philistines recognized that these plagues were coming from the God of Israel, and they returned the ark to Israel. They put the ark of the covenant on a cart, drawn by some cattle. When the ark came to the town of Beth-shemesh, some people opened the top of the ark to look inside. As a result, God instantly struck down some fifty thousand people!

I asked the Lord about the difference in the severity of judgment between the Philistines and the people in Beth-shemesh. His reply was that those with knowledge of the holy things, such as those who teach and minister the Word, are judged by a higher standard of accountability. It is no different than when two siblings are caught doing the same thing. The older child who knows better faces a more strict punishment than the one who is younger and does not know better.

The Lord also said, "When a person becomes familiar with 'the holy,' there is the danger of them taking it for granted. If taken for granted, there is the danger of that person mishandling the holy things of God. When a person mishandles and/or misappropriates the holy, there is the danger of divine judgment." We see an example of this in the New Testament when Ananias and his wife, Sapphira, sold some property and brought the money to the church where they laid it at the apostles' feet. The problem was that they lied and said the amount they brought was the whole amount they received for the property. In truth, they had kept back a portion of the money for themselves. (See Acts 5.) Rather than tell the truth, they lied. God judged them immediately for their sin and they both died instantly. We may think that this judgment was rather severe; however, when they sold their land and promised the proceeds to God for His work, it became holy. By lying about the amount to Peter, they touched what was holy. God's judgment did not mean there was a lack of love for them, any more than when a parent disciplines a child.

These examples show the importance God places on holy things. Moses mishandled his authority and relationship with God by doing what he wanted to do rather than obeying God's directive implicitly. Moses may have thought God would understand, but he mishandled what was holy.

Moses paid dearly for his disobedient, rash act. God's mercy, however, can be seen later when God allowed Moses to view the Promised Land from high atop a mountain. (See Deuteronomy 34:1–4.)

Our actions and lifestyle will either sanctify (or set God apart) in our lives in the eyes of others, or it will be a reproach to His holiness. What does your lifestyle say of your relationship with Him? Moses was not allowed to enter the Promised Land, though God did allow him to see it from the top of a mountain.

One last interesting fact about Moses is found in the New Testament in Matthew 17. Christ took three of His closest disciples with Him to a private place on top of a nearby mountain. There Christ was suddenly transfigured (transformed) before them. A bright light surrounded Him and two Old Testament people joined him. One was Elijah; the other was Moses. What a privilege it was to stand next to Christ and to speak with Him personally. This was the Christ; the One who had spoken to Moses from the burning bush. In the Old Testament when the Word says that an angel of the Lord showed up, it is usually referring to Christ. Although Moses was not permitted to step foot into the Promised Land, God still loved him and allowed him this special moment with Christ many hundreds of years later. Perhaps God gave Moses this moment because he had been used to show so many types and shadows of the Christ to come. At the time, Moses did not understand the symbolic nature of the tabernacle, but Christ was prepared to fulfill all of these types and shadows Moses had prophetically spoken of so many years earlier.

Just as Abraham left a legacy of friendship with God, Deuteronomy 34:10 tells us the legacy that Moses left: "And there arose not a prophet since in Israel like unto Moses, whom the LORD knew face to face." Such was the Father's love toward Moses that when Moses died, God buried him. (See Deuteronomy 34:6.)

Are you hungry for God? Do you hear Him calling your name? He is saying, "Come up to the mountain."

*"I have found David,
a man after mine own heart…"*
—Acts 13:22

CHAPTER 7

DAVID

After the Heart of God, Part I

It is one thing for people to acknowledge our relationship or walk with God, and quite another when God acknowledges or commends us. What God found in David so moved Him that we read, "In that day will I raise up the tabernacle of David that is fallen, and close up the breaches thereof; and I will raise up his ruins, and I will build it as in the days of old" (Amos 9:11). What was it about David's relationship with the Father that so moved Him? As we look at David's life, we see David's total abandonment to the worship of God. David is known as one of the greatest, if not the greatest, worshiper in history. To him, worship was not just something he did when he felt like it. To David, worship was a lifestyle to be lived out every day.

When you understand worship as a lifestyle, and not merely as a form that we are accustomed to here on earth, you will begin to understand that your life is to be worship unto God. Worship is more than just singing a love song unto God. It is more than simply raising your hands and adoring God. These things are the result of a worshiping heart, but they do not constitute worship in and of themselves. Jesus said, "True worshippers shall worship the Father in spirit and in truth" (John 4:23). When Jesus spoke this, He was telling the Samaritan woman at the well that worship is more than a physical action; it must flow from the depths of our being. It must become a lifestyle. Therefore, when I wake up, I am worshiping God. When I sleep, I am worshiping Him. Do I raise my hands and sing love songs to Him? Yes, but that is the result of a life sold out completely to Him. There are people who go through the motions every Sunday, but it means nothing. They are not worshipers, and they are not worshiping God.

The Father found in David something He had found in few others; it was a consuming, unquenchable desire for intimate communion with God. David worshiped the Father with everything within him because he was consumed with a love for the Father. So many people in our churches lift their hands and repeat the words on the screen, yet their hearts are far from Him. That is not worship; it is simply going through the motions. It may fool the people around them, but it does not fool God. Pure worship flows from the heart; it is lifting our hearts and spirits to God in complete surrender. It is doing so because we love Him, not because someone directs us to do so, or out of religious ritual. It was David who wrote, "My soul followeth hard after thee" (Ps. 63:8).

What we have seen in Moses' encounters with God's presence, as well as in the lives of others before him, we also witness in David's writings. As we study David's life, we will find that there is more insight into his intimate friendship with God in the psalms than there is in what we read in the history of David's life and reign. I love reading the psalms. Many beautiful worship songs that the church sings today were birthed in David and written into the psalms. I believe that David was inspired to write as he sat in God's presence, just adoring Him.

We get our first glimpse of David tending his father's

sheep. (See 1 Samuel 16.) This was a humble beginning for the person who would later become one of Israel's greatest kings. It is interesting to note that when God sent the prophet Samuel to the home of Jesse, David's father, to anoint the next king, his father did not even bother calling David in from the field. As Jesse passed all of his sons before Samuel, God kept telling the old prophet, "Not that one; not that one." Finally, after the seventh son was dismissed, Samuel looked at Jesse and asked if he had any other children. Almost as an afterthought, Jesse told the prophet that he indeed had one other son out in the field, tending sheep. How often have people thought, "If only somebody would acknowledge my calling or recognize God's hand on me, I could do great things for God." According to the pattern of David's life, God is the One who calls and raises people up. We will see in David's life that, despite the attempts of people to stop the plan of God, no one can keep God from fulfilling your destiny!

Even after David came in from the field and was anointed king, it would be many more years before he would assume the throne. (See 2 Samuel 2.) You may feel as though God has abandoned you or left you hanging out there in no man's land. You may have had a word spoken over your life, or God may have impressed upon you at some time a glimpse into your destiny. That may have been years ago when you were young. Now, perhaps, it may seem that God has forgotten you or the call upon your life. Let me tell you what we learn from the life of David: God has not forgotten you! If you are still in love with Him and walking with Him, then stand firm! Hang on! God will release you into your destiny! Life or your circumstances may seem hopeless. It may seem as though you are not going anywhere; however, in God's timetable, you will be brought forth. Do not despise small beginnings. Do not grow weary in well doing. If you will labor, in His time and His season, you will reap a precious harvest! This has been my personal experience as well.

Bible scholars tell us that from the time David was

anointed king until the day he was crowned king was between fourteen and twenty years. David did not become discouraged or anxious about the delay; he just continued to wait on God. God used this waiting period to intensify the relationship between Himself and David and to develop the leadership qualities David needed. Let me share something with you. There are people all over the world right now whom God has called for specific purposes and whom the church has yet to meet. They have been in the background waiting on God and developing an intimate friendship with Him. You may be one of them. You may feel as if what you sensed in your heart and spirit years ago may never come to fruition. You may think that the church does not know you exist. But God will release you. Just be patient! Wait on Him! Eagles take time to develop.

Just as an eagle does not learn to soar immediately after birth, neither do we learn to soar with the Father immediately after getting saved. It takes time for an eaglet to develop into a majestic eagle. You and I are put through a process of growth and maturity before we can soar like an eagle.

You may be familiar with one of David's first contacts with the throne of Israel, which came as a result of a war that was taking place between Israel and the Philistines. (See 1 Samuel 17.) David was sent to the front lines by his father to check on his brothers. While there, David heard the Philistine champion, Goliath, making threats against God's army. A holy anger arose in David when he heard the threats; so much so, that he began to question why no one had silenced the giant. It is a fact that the closer you get to God, the more holy anger you have against the enemy and against injustice. This is not the kind of anger in which you hold a grudge against a person or have bitterness toward someone. This is a righteous anger as demonstrated by Christ when He looked at the merchandisers in the temple. We read, "And Jesus went into the temple of God, and cast out all them that sold and bought in the temple, and overthrew the tables of the moneychangers, and the seats of them that sold doves, and said unto them, It is written, My house shall be called the house of prayer; but ye have made it a den of thieves" (Matt. 21:12–13). The Jews understood that prayer was their lifeline to God; it was the symbol of their relationship with Him. Their lives were centered on the temple, yet here, during Jesus' day, there was more selling and deal-making going on than worship to God. What rose up in Jesus should rise up in every true child of God when we look around us and see the body of Christ living below the standard God intended.

David looked at Goliath, then looked at the trembling, frightened, cowardly army of the Lord and became angry. He declared: "Who is this uncircumcised Philistine, that he should defy the armies of the living God?" (1 Sam. 17:26). When you walk with God and draw close to Him, you come to grasp His awesome power. Your life takes on a new boldness as you begin to see the Father as He really is—God Almighty, awesome in majesty and strength! When you come from His presence, you notice the ravages of the enemy and sin, and a holy anger will well up within you. You will look at other Christians who are struggling with depression, sickness, poverty or a host of other things, and you will cry out as David did, "Why do you permit the enemy to do this?"

The church in America puts up with too much garbage from the enemy. We allow the enemy to feed us one lie after another. He will say, "You will never change; your grandfather had this problem; your father had this problem; you will live with this the rest of your life." Foolishly, we cry in agreement with the enemy of our soul, the destroyer of our destiny. Rather than wimpishly agreeing, we should boldly proclaim the promises of God! When are God's children going to rise up, put their foot down and say, "Enough is enough—no more!" It amazes me how Christians react when I tell them, "You do not have to live with divorce, alcoholism, pornography, depression, anger or anything else the enemy throws at you." For many it comes as a revelation that they do not have to walk in the same path as those who came before them. They meekly carry their family curses, rather than seek divine help from the Bondage Breaker, Christ Himself. This tells me that we are spending more time entertaining our flesh and our selfish desires than we spend entertaining His presence. For in His presence we become free! It is not easy—in our microwave, get-it-done-quickly, pop-a-pill-for-everything-world—to change our worldly, unbiblical thinking and acting. We need, as God's children, to get back to spending time with Him alone. In doing so we, like David, can know how to deal with Goliaths that arise in our lives.

After David's bold statement, he was immediately taken to King Saul. What really disturbs me is how the seasoned soldiers of God preferred to allow David, a youth, handle Goliath alone, rather than stepping out on God's strength. How often does that happen today? We flock to hear those who have stepped beyond the veil and heard God's heartbeat, yet we fail to enter in ourselves. I am so hungry for God. What I desire, no other man or woman can satisfy, no matter how much they personally draw from the depths of His presence. Please do not misunderstand what I am saying; I love the messages of other ministers and purchase many videos and books. I thank God for those who are being used of Him. However, they cannot do for me what only God can do. They can only make me long to experience more of God for myself!

Unfortunately, many Christians are content to let their ministers or pastors pay the price to walk close to God. They are like little children reaping the benefits of parents who come back from a long trip; they hold out their hands in expectation, asking, "What did you bring for me? What new insight or revelation do you have for me today?" Without faulting these sincere leaders who do know God, all this does is produce kids of the King who know *about* Daddy, but who do not *know* Him.

When David told the army of Israel that Goliath should not be allowed to speak against the God of Israel, they all agreed.

Saul, at first, tried to talk David out of fighting Goliath. When that did not work, he attempted to get David to fight Goliath with his armor, his way. (See 1 Samuel 17:38.) We see similar things in the church today. We have a precious few who go after God, and when they come out of His presence with insight and revelation in what God is wanting to birth in the church, those with a Saul spirit come along and try to stop it. They either attempt to stop the birth all together or they try to harness it with their way of thinking.

Thankfully, David looked at Saul and replied, "King, I know what God is capable of doing. Just let me do it God's way." After two thousand years of our programs, our methods, getting our hands in it, you would think that we would have turned the world upside down by now. Unfortunately, that is not so. Instead of making disciples of Christ, we have made Baptists, Methodists, charismatics, Catholics, Pentecostals and many other "denominations." Imagine it, the church condemns genetic cloning, as it should, but look at what we have been doing for centuries! If that were not enough, we have divided into our own little camps and pointed at each other, saying who is right and who is wrong. While the church brags about a billion Christians on the earth, the church should hang its head in shame at the five billion who are still lost! Now, like David, the church has a real Goliath to contend with that threatens the army of the Lord. Islam is sweeping the globe. Who is going to stand up and face it? Perhaps the reason Jesus has appeared personally to Muslims in their dreams to witness to them is because the Davids of our generation are too busy seeing if Saul's armor will fit them.

After David declined Saul's offer, he went to face Goliath with only a slingshot and an unshakable faith in God. David's confidence was birthed out of experiences he had personally had with God. The psalms were written from time spent with God. And David knew that God had come through for him when he faced the lion and the bear and defeated them single-handedly. He knew that God would not fail him as he faced the giant! That was why Saul could not convince David that he was no match for Goliath. Nothing Saul said could cause David to question or doubt his own experience with the Father. David knew what God had done for him was real. God had shown Himself strong on David's account many times; now David was prepared to face Goliath unafraid, for he knew that God was with him.

Another aspect of David that we see is that he was not timid or anxious over the size of Goliath, nor did he exhibit any fear of him. Being in God's presence removes all traces of anxiety and fear. David had come to the realization of the bigness of His God. You just cannot argue with a person who has personally experienced God's faithfulness. There is a transformation that takes place within us as we spend time communing with God. It is not just a change of our lifestyle or even a change in our attitudes; it is a transformation of perspective—from ours to God's. The world around us, our family, friends, our workplace, and even life itself, look different when we spend time alone with God. As with Enoch, we can come into such intimacy with God that being with Him is more important than being with anyone else. Abraham became so acquainted with God that God began sharing things with him before He did them. Moses had communed so intently with God that his face glowed with God's presence. So there is a transformation in our outlook as well. Things that cause fear in others, will not cause us to fear. We can have peace in the midst of chaos! While everyone else is afraid of what the day will bring, we can walk in faith and peace that comes from God alone! Having spent time with God in the field, David was not afraid to face an enemy—no matter how big he appeared.

Every Christian will face a Goliath at some point in their lives. Like the Goliath that David faced, our Goliath wants nothing less than our complete destruction. Jesus said, "The thief comes to steal, kill, and to destroy" (John 10:10, author's paraphrase). Sounds like Goliath, does it not? Whoever or whatever your Goliath is, unless you destroy him, you will not move on toward your destiny. If David had run away in fear, Israel would not have achieved victory over the enemy. David, rather, chose to run toward his Goliath. He not only defeated him; he sealed his victory by cutting off Goliath's head with his own sword. David turned Goliath's own weapon against him. God allows us to do the same with our Goliaths. When we allow what the enemy has done to us to draw us closer to God, we are turning Satan's own weapons against him. What he tried to destroy us with, we, through God, can make stepping stones of faith!

Not only are there Goliaths that we face personally, but there are also Goliaths that have stood against the church. God is seeking a David to rise up to conquer and remove his head! It is quite possible that the Davids of our generation are not those whom the church elevates and promotes, much like the sons Jesse paraded before Samuel. The Davids of our generation are being found in the secret places, developing communion and a closeness with God. They are desirous of something that the world cannot offer. They have learned that the world and all its allure cannot compare to their relationship and communion with God.

Their solitude in the secret place in sweet fellowship with God has resulted in such a transformation in their outlook that as God begins to bring them out of the secret place to be used of Him, the church will be amazed. Perhaps the church will not be as amazed at the anointing on their lives as that these men and women of God do not resemble those who came before them. These new Davids will be people who do not crave the accolades of their peers. They will not care for the opinions of those around them or whether their audiences are impressed. These individuals will be consumed only with God's opinion of them. They will not be as concerned with the sanctified saints as they are with those who have been so neglected by the church—the lost, the destitute, the alcoholic, the prostitute. They will seek to serve and minister to those on the highways and byways of life; the ones the church did not want to embrace.

Many of our ministers today are so caught up with position and status that God cannot use them to the degree He desires. You may remember Paul's sharp rebuke of Peter one day as Jewish and gentile believers were enjoying a fellowship meal together. Peter, wanting to save face, removed himself from the gentiles so as not to look bad among his Jewish friends. Paul was quick to expose this wrong and confronted Peter openly. (See Galatians 2:11–12.) Can you imagine what would happen in a room of ministers and believers if one of them called the other out in front of everyone? Yet, Paul told Timothy, "Them that sin rebuke before all, that others also may fear" (1 Tim. 5:20). What Peter did was clearly wrong. God does not show partiality; neither should His ministers or any person who is a Christian.

Following the defeat of Goliath and the Philistines, David gained sudden popularity. Despite the applause, the accolades and even the songs written about him, however, David kept himself humble. About this same time David was summoned before King Saul to play music to soothe the troubled king. You may recall that Saul was vexed in his spirit because the Spirit of God had left him, and an evil, tormenting spirit filled the void. (See 1 Samuel 16.) This was the direct result of Saul's rebellion and disobedience. Saul's life should remind us that, despite God's hand being laid on us, if we willfully turn away in disobedience, God will remove His hand from our lives.

David was apparently well known for his anointed music; therefore, when the king needed a minstrel, David was summoned. As David played on his instrument, the evil spirit that dwelt in Saul could not bear it and departed for a time. It was not just the music itself that drove away the evil spirit; it was the atmosphere the music created. David would later write, "But thou art holy, O thou that inhabitest the praises of Israel" (Ps. 22:3). Just as with our praise, it is not so much the words as it is that He dwells in the midst of our praise. We see this demonstrated in the life of Jeshoshaphat. (See 2 Chronicles 20.) Prior to going out to battle, God instructed Jehoshaphat to place the singers in the front. They were to go before the army. God was going to fight the battle for them and wanted them to worship and praise as they marched.

David's music was anointed because David walked with God, and God touched David's music with His presence. As I mentioned earlier, the anointing as a "divine enabling" on a person's life does not mean that person has a special closeness with God. When God calls a person, He anoints them for a particular task and he or she will receive the ability to complete it. However, it is our hunger for God that determines the level or degree of our relationship with Him. Drawing close to Him brings a person into a deeper dimension of relationship. Of course, that deeper relationship will impact the anointing in a positive way. We look at the person and think, "He has a heavy anointing or greater anointing on him than others do." That is not so. There are not degrees to the anointing, only degrees to the relationship level. The closer you get to God, the less is seen of you and the more is seen of Him. The more that God is allowed to dwell in us, the more the anointing flows through us unhindered. When we hear an anointed song or message that seems deeper or more anointed than other messages or songs, it's really the result of that person having stepped aside and let God flow freely through them.

When we compare the majority of believers today to those of the early church as seen in the book of Acts, we fall short. Despite our having available Christian books, Bibles, teachers and a host of other things, we are not walking in the level of authority in which the early church walked. Although this has become somewhat of a pet peeve for me, I must be honest and say that I am also guilty of falling so short of the mark. I believe there is a simple explanation for such a vast difference between the modern-day church and the early church. As we cited earlier, the apostle John writes, "And they loved not their lives unto the death" (Rev. 12:11). The priority for the early church was Christ alone. They did not care for this life as we usually do. There is nothing wrong with enjoying life, but they did not hold to this life as dearly as we do. As seen in the book of Acts, the early church was focused on fellowshiping with one another and winning their world. When a person has an unquenchable love for God and does not fear death, they will go anywhere without worrying or being fearful. They will boldly face the enemy and proclaim the good news. What did they have to lose? Paul said, "We are confident, I say, and willing rather to be absent from the body, and to be present with the Lord" (2 Cor. 5:8, author's paraphrase). The life that awaits us is beyond our comprehension and understanding.

Why do so many allow life to hold them so tightly when as Christians we are only passing through? We are pilgrims and strangers here in this world, having something far better awaiting us when we leave. We are just visitors staying for awhile before Christ calls us home. That is not to say that we should stop making plans and just sit back and take our ease. On the contrary, we are to be diligently about the Father's business. There is nothing wrong with possessing cars, homes and nice things as long as these things do not possess us. That is one of the differences between the modern-day church and the early church. The early church was focused on spreading the gospel and not on building personal kingdoms. To hear some ministers today at our "success" seminars, you would think Christ was going to set up His kingdom next to ours, rather than destroy the earth and redo it by fire as He foretold. Please do not misunderstand me. I do not think that it is wrong to own things or to be successful in business or ministry. In fact, we should be successful in business and ministry. We are to be blessed as His children. We, however, need to keep all things in perspective. The purpose of being blessed financially is so that we can be a blessing and can finance God's agenda. David was one of the most blessed of the kings of Israel, yet from his writings we know that he never lost his desire to be in God's presence. David knew that in His presence was fullness of joy, and at His right hand are pleasures for evermore (Ps. 16:11).

Although David was not perfect in his walk with God and went through some difficult times, he maintained a deep love for God. It is important that you maintain closeness with the Father all the time. Once you taste of His presence, that level must be maintained and even built upon. The apostle James wrote, "Draw close to God and He will draw close to you" (James 4:8, author's paraphrase). I have read accounts of ministers who no longer walked with God after enjoying years of fellowship with Him. Their falling away was usually preceded by a traumatic event or situation in their lives. David faced such an event in His life. While David and his army were away fighting the enemy, they returned to their camp to find that their wives and children had been taken captive. They became so distraught that David's men became angry with David and turned on him. (See 1 Samuel 30.) Many Christians would have immediately retreated to the nearest psychologist or surrendered to a mental breakdown. But not David. The scripture declares: "But David encouraged himself in the LORD his God" (1 Sam. 30:6). Then David was able to think clearly and he immediately sought guidance from the Lord. He had confidence in the relationship he had cultivated for years with God.

Life can be painful. No one is completely immune from pain because we live in an imperfect and sin-sick world. Like David, we need to close ourselves in with the Lord when we are faced with a bad situation or any situation that we cannot handle. When we do so, God is able to speak to us in a clear voice with the guidance we need. Any time my wife and I are faced with a situation where we do not know what to do, we make it a point to stop whatever we are doing and wait upon God. David knew the importance of being still. It is not always easy to be still when we are facing a crisis, but again it is David who wrote, "Be still, and know that I am God" (Ps. 46:10). The enemy tries to take advantage of a crisis by overloading our mind with demonic thoughts of worry and anxiety. God says, "Be still, My child, and know that I am God!"

Another example of the ways a crisis affects us can be

seen in the life of Job. After he lost everything, including his children and his riches, Job no doubt had a lot on his mind. His wife came to him and said, "Why don't you just curse God and die?" Her pain and anger was understandable for she too had lost much. Job's response has become well known; he replied, "Thou speakest as one of the foolish women speaketh. What? Shall we receive good at the hand of God, and shall we not receive evil? In all this did not Job sin with his lips" (Job 2:10). We, as Christians, need to keep in mind that although God is ultimately in control, we live in a fallen world that has been cursed. As free moral agents, we have the choice of how we deal with crisis. Will we, like Job's wife, blame God and curse Him or will we, by faith, trust in His providence? Will we listen to well-meaning friends who do not help the situation, or will we trust Him? I believe, as many others do, that everything is "Father filtered." This means that nothing happens to us that God does not either allow or cause. He is sovereign in His wisdom and actions! God is in control. We may not always understand or see His hand in the situation; nevertheless, He is in control. It is true that some things which happen to us are the result of our bad choices or occur because we have given opportunities to the enemy. For example, if a man drinks too much and drives his car into a tree, he cannot blame God and say, "Why did You allow this?" That would be foolish! God, in His grace and mercy has promised us, "all things work together for good to them that love God, to them who are the called according to his purpose" (Rom. 8:28). What an exciting promise! God promises to turn even our mistakes into good if only we will love Him and live according to His will and purpose!

After seeking God and hearing an answer from Him, David pursued those who kidnapped his loved ones and recovered everything. Would the results have been the same if David had acted rashly, without consulting God, pursuing the enemy without the blessing of God? Probably not. Situations such as these in David's life served only to strengthen his relationship with God and his unwavering faith in God. God proved Himself over and over again in David's life. If, like David, you are going through a traumatic situation right now, stop what you are doing and encourage yourself in the Lord. Follow the scriptural admonition: "But ye, beloved, building up yourselves on your most holy faith, praying in the Holy Ghost, Keep yourselves in the love of God, looking for the mercy of our Lord Jesus Christ unto eternal life" (Jude 20–21). We are to build ourselves up on our most holy faith and to keep ourselves in the love of God. You might be asking right now, "How can a person do that? How can I do that?" You simply need to shut off everything around you, and, as Paul said, "[Speak] to yourselves in psalms and hymns and spiritual songs, singing and making melody in your heart to the Lord" (Eph. 5:19). As you open your heart wide, singing love songs and pouring out your heart to Him, God will take you in His arms, hold you tightly and let you know that you are His child and that everything is going to be okay. Never lose sight of the promise that God knows what you are going through, and, despite what you are facing, God has not left you. The enemy will lie to you saying, "It is all over; you are through!" Not so—God sees you right where you are. Be still and know that He is God!

David's journey to his destiny was not easy nor was it short. There were times in his life when he must have wondered if he would live to see his promised destiny. Some of those times were while he was playing music for Saul. (Saul threw his spear at David, trying to kill him, while he was playing music for him; see 1 Samuel 18:9–10.) A person outside the protection of God will continually sink deeper and deeper into satanic bondage, as Saul did. The greater his bondage became, the more hatred for David filled his heart. Just as our love relationship with God is progressive, in that it continues to grow, the opposite is true with the enemy. Saul continued to regress under the hateful influences of the enemy. Rather than repenting and seeking God, he continued to spiral downward into the emotional abyss of depression and rage. We see that today when people turn from God, they move away from Him. It begins with a little step, but it continues until they no longer can feel Him tugging at their hearts.

Saul knew that David was anointed king, so he hated him even more. Because of Saul's hatred, David was forced to flee for his life. He was always looking over his shoulder, not knowing when Saul's soldiers would catch up to him. During this perilous time, David fled to the cave of Adullam. (See 1 Samuel 22.) It is amazing how God will still use a person, even during times of crisis and even when they cannot understand what is happening to them. While in the cave of Adullam, we are told men who were in debt and discouraged gathered themselves around David. They were not looking for sympathy or help. They were drawn to David because there was just something about him. I believe it was more than just recognizing God's hand on David. I believe what drew them was the Father's fragrance. Perhaps it was not a literal fragrance that they could smell, but an inner fragrance of a life touched by God. Although David did not understand everything he was going through, God was using him even during this time to bring hope and encouragement to others.

Just because we do not understand why we are going through painful circumstances does not mean that God is not working in our lives. God was still at work in David's life. Of the four hundred who joined David in that dismal cave, thirty would become known as David's mighty men. David may have been running for his life, but God was using this period as an opportunity to train him and to use him to train others for leadership. During the time David was on the run, he walked in integrity toward God's anointed leadership, even though Saul was trying to kill him. (See 1 Samuel 24.) Although opportunities arose, he refused to take Saul's life. This is evidence that David did not lose his sensitivity to God; he continued to enjoy fellowship with Him even in the midst of adverse circumstances.

David's life shows us the faithfulness of God in bringing

to pass what He has promised, even when it seems the opposite of those promises is happening. As you read the Psalms, it is easy to see the times when David appeared to bend under the pressure of living in hiding. Yet we also see in those same Psalms, David's resolve to keep sight of his closeness with God or His hand upon him. David wrote, "He brought me up also out of a horrible pit, out of the miry clay, and set my feet upon a rock, and established my goings" (Ps. 40:2). Psalm 23 is one of the most well-known and beloved of David's psalms. David wrote in verse 4, "Yea, though I walk through the valley of the shadow of death, I will fear no evil: for thou art with me; thy rod and thy staff they comfort me." David lived in the shadow of death often while he was running from Saul. He had learned first-hand not to fear what men could do to him; that is because of His relationship with His Shepherd.

The day finally came when Saul died in the midst of a battle. (See 1 Samuel 31.) Though David was now free from Saul's hatred, it would still be more than seven years before he would become king over all of Israel. (See 2 Samuel 2.) After the death of Saul, the tribe of Judah crowned David king, and he began to rule at Hebron. Hebron was not exactly paradise; yet, again, it was part of God's plan in raising David up. Your "Hebron" might be teaching a small-group class or working in a ministry, knowing that God has promised a greater destiny than your present sphere of influence. Working in the nursery or leading a small class is not insignificant, but if a person is called to a larger ministry, starting small can be difficult. God uses these times to train us and prepare us.

When I was in my late teens, I knew I was called to some day preach the gospel. However, until a few years ago, God had me doing everything from janitorial work in the church to teaching a small Sunday school class. I will be honest with you; in retrospect I would not trade those times for anything. Though it was difficult and lonely, God taught me many important lessons during those years. I held every position possible in a church before stepping into a pastoral

role. Even now, while we are members of a dynamic and
growing church, we patiently wait for what God has in store
for us next. While I'm waiting, I am busy working within
the church. I not only preach when called upon, but I have
also taught classes and have been involved in street ministry.
My wife and I have learned during this time to wait upon
God and to let Him complete in us what is necessary in
order for us to step into the fullness of our promised destiny.

As you look at David's life, there is no indication that he
became impatient while reigning in Hebron. During this
time, David learned to forgive those who were his enemies
under Saul's leadership. Had it not been for the incredible
relationship David had with God, he would have surely
failed under the pressure of running for his life. That relationship was not cultivated in a day; nor was it first cultivated in the cave. It is during life's most difficult crises that
we will be grateful for the intimate relationship we have cultivated with God during more peaceful times.

Do you feel Him tugging at your heart? The Father longs
for each of us to experience an intimate relationship with
Him; not just a duplicate of what David had, but a personal
and unique walk with Him. There is a place in His presence
where you are aware of nothing but Him. That is the place
He is leading you and me. That is the place He longs for His
body, the church, to enter into. Nothing else seems important in His presence; everything else pales in comparison to
Him. He is sweeter than honey, more precious than gold,
purer than silver; He is altogether lovely. And you know
what? He is my Lover and Friend, my closest Companion.
And He longs for you to know Him intimately. Follow
David's footsteps; enter through worship. There is sweet
communion awaiting all who enter His secret place. Let
your hunger overwhelm you until you are consumed with a
burning desire for only Him.

"I have found David,
a man after mine own heart…"
—ACTS 13:22

CHAPTER 8

DAVID

After the Heart of God, Part II

Shortly after becoming king over all of Israel, more than seven years after he began reigning in Hebron, David desired to bring the ark of the covenant to Jerusalem. (See 2 Samuel 6.) The ark, which Israel had lost to the Philistines many years earlier, had been returned to them and kept at the home of an Israelite, Abinadab, for twenty years (1 Samuel 7:1–2). The negligence of Saul regarding the ark of the covenant, the symbol of God's presence, gives us greater insight into the kind of person Saul was; he never once considered bringing the ark back to its rightful place as the center of Israel's worship.

In contrast, when David was crowned king, the first thing he wanted to do was reestablish the presence of God to its rightful position. Praise God that there are people today who are hungry to see the presence of God restored to the church; they want the Lord to repossess His church and show Himself powerful with signs and wonders as He did in the book of Acts. David called thirty thousand mighty men to gather in procession to bring the ark back to Jerusalem. After placing the ark on a new cart, they began the jubilant journey to Jerusalem. As they walked, music played and the people rejoiced.

However, you may recall that the jubilant procession turned tragic as they reached the place called Nachon's threshing floor. It was there the oxen stumbled and Uzzah, son of Abinadab, reached out to steady the ark, touching it unlawfully. God killed him instantly. What had begun with enthusiasm, ended in tragedy. Some may think that the severity of God's punishment was unwarranted. After all, Uzzah was just being helpful. However we need to understand that Uzzah was guilty of mishandling the holy thing of God. For twenty years Uzzah had seen the ark every day inside his father's home. We can safely assume that Uzzah knew the history of the ark's journey through the wilderness and how it also came to be placed in his home. It is also safe to assume that in growing up around the ark, Uzzah became familiar with it and no doubt was accustomed to sitting in its presence. Perhaps that familiarity caused Uzzah to take God for granted, and in doing so, he mishandled the holy. Knowing the holiness of God, Uzzah should have known not to touch the ark. When we become too familiar with something, we are often in danger of mishandling it. Perhaps he thought God needed his help. God did not need Uzzah's help.

Of course, if the ark had been transported in the manner that God ordained, Uzzah's life would not have been endangered. However, the death of Uzzah ended the procession to Jerusalem and caused fear to come upon David. David placed the ark at the home of Obed-edom, where it stayed for three months while he returned to Jerusalem to reconsider his plans to return the ark to Jerusalem. David was left to figure out what went wrong.

During the three months the ark remained at the home of Obed-edom, word came to David that God was blessing Obed-edom and his household. Meanwhile, David was studying the Scriptures to discover the proper way to transport the ark. He discovered God's divine instructions for bringing His presence home again. Once again, David began the journey to bring the ark to Jerusalem. However, this time was different. In David's first attempt, he had tried to do it his way; now he was doing it God's way. This time the priests bore the ark on their shoulders, just as they had done in the days of Moses. Every six steps, they stopped and offered a sacrifice to God in praise and worship.

We must learn a lesson from David's mistake. If we as the church are going to see the manifest presence of God in our churches, we are going to have to do it God's way, not our way. This requires that we find out what God wants to do and how He wants to do it. Then we must determine to flow with Him. God moves in His time and His way. You and I need only to flow with Him as we seek to understand His ways.

After David began the procession to Jerusalem, they played music and David danced before the ark of His presence. David, like those before him who enjoyed close communion with God, did not care about the opinions of others. As the street party entered Jerusalem, David's wife, Michal, looked out the window and saw David dancing mightily before the ark, oblivious to the presence or opinions of those around him. Seeing David dancing upset Michal so much that the scripture says she despised him in her heart.

There are those in the church who, like Michal, despise those who desire to worship God with their whole heart and abandon their lives to Him. This spirit of Michal can be found throughout church history in people who despise the "new" move of God and look down on the freedom of expression of a person in relationship with Him. How sad it is when people who call themselves Christians judge the freedom of expression in another person's life, only because it does not fit in their theological "box." If my expression of praise and worship to the Father offends someone, I will not apologize. I gave my all to the devil in foolish "expressions" when I was hopelessly lost, and I will give my all now to the

One who has so mercifully saved me! As long as my walk with the Father does not violate the known will of God as revealed in the Word of God, I do not really care what people may think or say. I am not in this to win anyone's approval; I am in it to win Him!

The church my wife and I attend is very Pentecostal in its expressive praise and worship, as well as in the ministry of the Word. We have freedom in our church to express our love to Christ as we choose. If you were to visit our church, two things would be evident: the heavy presence of God and the people's total abandonment to Him as expressed by our praise and worship. You would see some dancing before the Lord; others might be lying quietly before Him. Some may be crying while others are laughing. Yet each in his or her own way is expressing love for Christ as they respond to His presence. It amazes me that some of our visitors focus their attention on the "worship expressions," despising the worshipers, instead of focusing on the holy presence of the Father.

God's response to Michal's attitude toward David's worship was severe. Because she despised David she became barren, which was considered a curse for women. This Hebrew word for *despise* meant to "dis-esteem, to consider contemptible and to scorn." Did Michal scorn David? No, she loved him, but she scorned his worship and ultimately, the relationship he enjoyed with God.

People who despise those who are unashamedly "lost" in worship and praise are in effect despising God. It is similar to the Pharisees of Jesus' day who looked upon His miracles and ministry and despised Him. Christ's evaluation of their attitude was that they did not know God. I know there are some people who do not understand the Spirit-filled life, and how such a life will impact their walk with God. Those people may question worship expressions they see in church; they may even reject them. But their response is more out of ignorance than the rebellious spirit of Michal.

On the other hand, there are those, like Michal, who live in the king's home and yet despise those who worship God with all their might. They do not attempt to understand the manifestations taking place in church; instead, they question the validity of these people's relationships with God. When a person despises those who choose to lose themselves in worship to God, they are in danger of becoming spiritually "barren" and unfruitful.

I believe as it was with the Pharisees of Jesus' day, so it is now with modern-day "despisers." They have no relationship with God because they do not know Him. This statement may offend some people, but if the spirit of Michal is allowed to invade our churches, it could kill the move of God taking place in our churches.

When Michal confronted David about his actions before the people, he responded, "It was before the LORD, which chose me before thy father, and before all his house, to appoint me ruler over the people of the LORD, over Israel: therefore will I play before the LORD. And I will yet be more vile than thus, and will be base in mine own sight: and of the maidservants which thou hast spoken of, of them shall I be had in honour" (2 Sam. 6:21–22). David declared that God had been too good to him for him to care what people thought; he was going to unashamedly and unreservedly worship Him! The purpose of the spirit of Michal is to stop and kill the free expression of love toward God. Many churches are so regimented in their expressions of praise and worship that God will not visit them with His presence. God has chosen to limit Himself to the choices of our free will; He wants us to choose to worship Him out of our love for Him.

Perhaps some of Michal's anger was based in fear of consequences that David's actions could cause. As royalty, perhaps she did not think it was appropriate for the king to show such unrestrained emotion in front of others, especially laying aside his royal robes. Michal was more concerned with what others would say than with how God would enjoy such worship. Some people who despise the free expression of love and worship of God are also concerned with the opinions of others more than the opinion of the One who counts.

If you ask them why they are upset, they usually have no definable argument. They simply say, "I don't think they should do that" or "Why do they act that way? Why cry out? Why so expressive?"

Perhaps, like David, you feel the Spirit tugging at your heart to let yourself freely express your love toward God, but you are concerned about what others may think. Let me encourage you. Like David, God has been too good to you for you not to express your love toward Him in unashamed and unrestrained praise and worship. You do not have to be as loud and expressive as David, although you may be. Just step out and give your all to the One who gave His all for you. The scripture says that if we are ashamed of Him, He will be ashamed of us. (See Luke 9:26.) David would later write clear instructions for exuberant praise to God:

> Praise ye the Lord. Praise God in his sanctuary: praise him in the firmament of his power. Praise him for his mighty acts: praise him according to his excellent greatness. Praise him with the sound of the trumpet: praise him with the psaltery and harp. Praise him with the timbrel and dance: praise him with stringed instruments and organs. Praise him upon the loud cymbals: praise him upon the high sounding cymbals. Let every thing that hath breath praise the Lord. Praise ye the Lord.
>
> —Psalm 150

David, under the inspiration of the Holy Spirit, commanded everyone to praise the Lord.

I find it interesting that the modern-day "Michals" who despise the free expression of worship to God say very similar things as Michal said to David. Michal berated David, saying: "How glorious was the king of Israel today, who uncovered himself today in the eyes of the handmaids of his servants, as one of the vain fellows shamelessly uncovereth himself!" (2 Sam. 6:20). She criticized him for the way he was acting in front of everyone. Today, these "Michals" will usually say something like, "Well, that person doesn't have to dance like that," or, "That person shouldn't be so loud." They are actually despising in their hearts the freedom of worshipful expression. These same people would not consider it strange to shout and high five everyone near them during a sports game. Others, at the birth of their baby, will freely cry for joy. Still others, at the announcement of some good news, will let out a shout. Yet for some strange reason, many church people do not get happy or enthusiastic in their worship of God. For myself, I refuse not to express to Him my love and joy. God has done too much for me not to raise my voice and get happy when I praise Him.

The Gospel according to Luke records an incident in the life of Christ when a woman expressed her love to Christ in a way that made those around Him uncomfortable and upset. We read in Luke 7:37–39:

> And, behold, a woman in the city, which was a sinner, when she knew that Jesus sat at meat in the Pharisee's house, brought an alabaster box of ointment, And stood at his feet behind him weeping, and began to wash his feet with tears, and did wipe them with the hairs of her head, and kissed his feet, and anointed them with the ointment. Now when the Pharisee which had bidden him saw it, he spake within himself, saying, This man, if he were a prophet, would have known who and what manner of woman this is that toucheth him: for she is a sinner.

I love Jesus' response to their remarks, He said:

> Simon, Seest thou this woman? I entered into thine house, thou gavest me no water for my feet: but she hath washed my feet with tears, and wiped them with the hairs of her head. Thou gavest me no kiss: but this woman since the time I came in hath not ceased to kiss my feet. My head with oil thou didst not anoint: but this woman hath anointed my feet with ointment. Wherefore I say unto thee, Her

sins, which are many, are forgiven; for she loved
much: but to whom little is forgiven, the same
loveth little (v. 44–47).

Do not be like Michal. Do not despise the way people
respond to God in expressing their love for Him through
praise and worship. Instead, choose to allow yourself to
become as David when he brought the ark into the city—
praise God with unrestrained joy! If people look at you differently or question you, just respond as David did. God has
been too good for you not to worship Him freely, giving Him
your all.

Once the ark of the covenant was back in Jerusalem, it
was placed under the tent that David had pitched for it.
Bible scholars believe that the ark was not placed into the
tabernacle that Moses constructed for it, where only the
high priest could enter the presence of the ark once a year
to atone for Israel's sin. That tabernacle remained in the city
of Gibeon, according to 2 Chronicles 1:13. Some people
believe that when the ark was placed under the tent that
David had pitched for it, everyone had access to the presence of God there. While the scriptures are not clear concerning this view, if it is correct, I can understand David's
reasoning for placing it in such a manner. David had such a
hunger for God and enjoyed His presence so much that he
would naturally want everyone to enjoy the same kind of
fellowship and communion that he experienced.

We are told in 1 Chronicles 16:37, "So he left there before
the ark of the covenant of the LORD, Asaph and his brethren,
to minister before the ark continually, as every day's work
required." David's love for the Father was so strong that he
wanted continuous praise and worship to be offered up to
the Father. Imagine what it was like to go to sleep with the
sound of worship and praise ringing in the distance. Then
imagine waking in the morning to the sound of praise and
worship. This would be the perfect start for the day.

Why should it be any different for us today? God longs for
us to praise and worship Him all the time. Worship and

praise should be a lifestyle, not just something we do in church on Sundays. When I lose myself in praise and worship, my day goes better and I am more refreshed. I still accomplish my daily tasks, but I am continually either verbally singing praise to God or singing within my heart. When we do that, people notice something different about us. There is a glow of God's presence that exudes from our life. I do not think the Father gets any greater joy than from a child of His freely praising and worshiping Him.

I am so conscious of His nearness at times that I sense His presence everywhere I go. I was walking into a grocery store one day, and as I walked to the glass doors, I was communing with God. When I got to the automatic doors, I paused and said, "You first, Lord." That may sound a little strange, but there is a relationship with the Father in which talking with Him is no different than speaking to someone else, except for the level of conversation. I would rather spend five minutes in His presence talking with Him, than a lifetime talking to anyone else. Knowing how much the Father wants to speak and commune with us, why settle for anything less? David refused to settle for less; neither should you.

Do you hunger for God? Do you long for that place of continuous worship and communion? Are you willing to abandon yourself to do His will? For the one who does, Jesus promised, "He who has My commandments and keeps them, it is he who loves Me. And he who loves Me will be loved by My Father, and I will love him and will manifest Myself to him" (John 14:21, author's paraphrase). That Greek word for *manifest* means "to show oneself, to come to view, and to appear"! The intimate relationship with God that we long for is real. The Lord will manifest Himself to us. Just how hungry are you? Do you long for Him more than any other? He longs for you even more than you long for Him. The Father loves us with a deep consuming love. Reach out to Him and He will take you by the hand and lead you into His presence. As you lose yourself in worship, He will take you in His arms and draw you closer.

Having reviewed David's priority of bringing the presence of God to the nation will give us a greater appreciation for some of his psalms. To really understand the level of intimacy that David enjoyed with the Lord requires that we read some of David's love letters to Him. These love letters give us much insight into David's relationship with God. Only a truly hungry person can appreciate the depth of the worshiping heart of David. As we have seen already, his lifestyle was one of total abandonment to the Father. You and I must choose that abandonment to Him if we are to enjoy the level of fellowship and communion that God intended for us to have since the Garden of Eden.

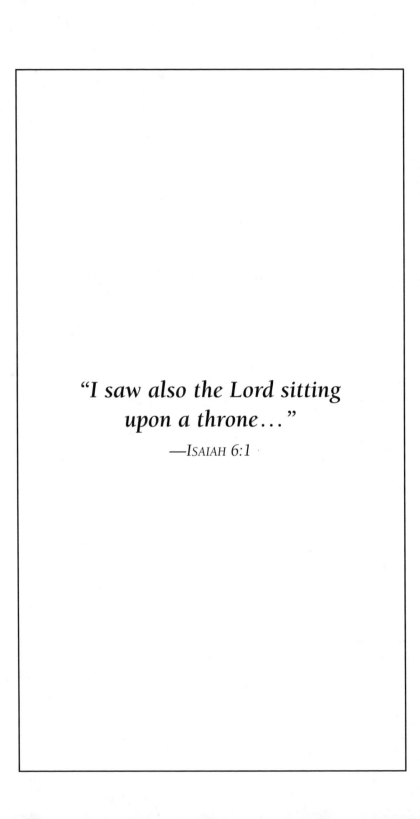

*"I saw also the Lord sitting
upon a throne…"*

—Isaiah 6:1

CHAPTER 9

ISAIAH

Glimpses of the Throne

It is interesting to note that the book of Isaiah spoke so prophetically of Christ and the End Times. Christ, Himself, also quoted from Isaiah on a number of occasions. From all evidence, Isaiah, the prophet of God, was considered a righteous man. It is important to understand this because to be used of God as Isaiah was, required that he be righteous, at least from the standpoint of the law. Isaiah was a mighty prophet during a period of time in Israel that saw the hand of God moving against His beloved people for their sins. Yet in the midst of this chaos and sin, Isaiah comes on the scene with a hunger and desire for God like few before him. No matter how bad things may get around us, God will always have people who will depend upon Him and long for Him. As you read through the Book of Isaiah you find that God has not forgotten His people despite their forgetting Him. God always seems to have someone who will come along beside Him and declare His heart. That is what Isaiah does, and the things God reveals to Him still minister to us today.

As we have seen in previous chapters, God reveals much in the secret place. What insight and knowledge is yet to be found in the secret place, that place of being alone with Him? When is the last time you got away from the distractions of life and just got alone with the Father either in your closet or the front room, or closed your bedroom door and knelt at your bed and poured out your heart to Him? It is when we are alone, in those places of quietness, the secret place that God really begins to speak to our heart.

Some of the most beautiful prophecies concerning the coming of Christ and His life are found in the book of Isaiah. To fully grasp some of the things Isaiah said, we need to understand the depth of Isaiah's relationship with the Father. Just as with King David, we can get a glimpse into Isaiah's heart when we read some of the things he wrote. Isaiah's words continue to speak to us today, thousands of years after his words were recorded, because God revealed His words to Isaiah as he walked with Him. God gave this prophet a wonderful glimpse into the spiritual realm that few before or since have experienced. One of these experiences, recorded in Isaiah 6, is an awesome vision that God gave him. He wrote, "I saw also the LORD, sitting upon a throne, high and lifted up, and his train filled the temple" (v. 1). What a magnificent sight this must have been! Isaiah describes the robe that God wore as it filled the entire temple. As if that sight were not enough, Isaiah went on to describe what was happening around the throne: "Above it stood the seraphims: each one had six wings; with twain he covered his face, and with twain he covered his feet, and with twain he did fly" (v. 2). Perhaps you question the significance of the angelic beings covering their faces and their feet. We read as well of others who catch a glimpse of God but are not able to look upon Him. I believe the reason for this is that no one, other than Christ, is worthy to look upon the face of God. We know, of course, that the day will come when we will stand before Him and look upon Him. So it is not so much that we cannot, as it is that we are not yet worthy to do so. I cannot wait to get to heaven to behold the face of Him who has captured my heart and life! What a time that will be to gaze into the eyes of Him who searched me out and desired to know me. Can you imagine the awesome depths of those eyes? Perhaps that is why people and angels cannot gaze upon Him. That penetrating look, that holy gaze coming from the throne of God, is too much to bear. To see the depth of love and desire He would express in that look would be too much for us to handle! Perhaps we can relate that power of expression to the scripture where we read, "Turn away thine eyes from me, for they have overcome me" (Song of Sol. 6:5). His gaze is too powerful; it is as if He is looking right through us—because He is. Nothing is hidden from His gaze. Praise God for sending Jesus Christ, for only through His shed blood are we made worthy to stand before God, the Father! All that I am, all that I desire to be, all that I will become is all because of Him. Some people mistakenly believe that God would never permit them to go beyond the veil or to draw near to Him. It is true that we cannot do so on our own merits, but He welcomes us with open arms on the merits of Christ and His shed blood. So how hungry are you? Do you want Him more than anything and anyone else?

Isaiah continued to describe his vision: "And one cried unto another, and said, Holy, holy, holy, is the LORD of hosts: the whole earth is full of his glory" (Isa. 6:3). You can search throughout the Scriptures, and you will never find the angels repeating anything else about the totality of the nature of the Father, as you see here. They cried out, "Holy, holy, holy!" The Bible tells us that without holiness, no one will see the Lord. (See Hebrews 12:14.) This passage is interesting because the angels could have cried, "God is love," or "God is merciful and just!" We know that God is all these things and many more; but the angels cried repeatedly, "He is holy! He is holy!" They sum up His attributes in the word *holy.* Because the phrase is repeated over and over, it is meant to communicate the significance of this quality.

Holiness has mistakenly been taught by some as a strict regime of do's and don'ts. Most of the teaching on holiness has been centered and focused on the external, such as what you wear and where you hang out. To be honest, adding rules or codes of conduct to your lifestyle does not make you holy. Holiness is a quality of purity and "rightness" before God that must be birthed in the heart and lived out in our lives. Holiness is an internal issue that affects our external lifestyles. The church has erred in trying to legislate pious rules of holiness, rather than allowing the Holy Spirit to work in individual lives. Yes, there are certain standards in the Word of God that all Christians should practice, but we should not split hairs over trivial matters. If God has convicted you of an attitude or action or other issue of lifestyle, then follow the guidance of the Holy Spirit in your heart. But do not make that "standard" a doctrine and demand that others follow your path. Do not judge them as wrong; allow the Holy Spirit to do His marvelous work in their lives, just as He is doing in your life.

The angels exalt our awesome God by declaring His holiness continually before His throne. While I long to be holy as He is holy, I realize that only through the power of the Spirit will this ever happen. My desire is not based on a human idea of holiness, but rather on God's idea of holiness for us, which can only come through revelation by the Holy Spirit.

Isaiah continued to describe his vision, "And the posts of the door moved at the voice of him that cried, and the house was filled with smoke. Then said I, Woe is me! for I am undone; because I am a man of unclean lips, and I dwell in the midst of a people of unclean lips: for mine eyes have seen the King, the LORD of hosts" (Isa. 6:4–5). Just as it happened with others who have had an encounter with God, Isaiah became acutely aware of his sin in the light of God's holiness. As I mentioned earlier, Isaiah was, by all accounts, a righteous person according to the law of Moses. Yet, when his flesh encountered Deity, when he came face to face with divine purity, with holiness, Isaiah cried out, "Woe is me!"

This will always be the reaction when we encounter God. No matter how intimate our walk with Him seems to be, when He reveals Himself in a greater way, we again sense our unworthiness, our sin. It is no wonder the Hebrews believed that to see God was to incur an immediate death sentence.

I have often wondered how people can sit in the back pew in our churches today and resist the moving of the Spirit during an altar call. One day, while praying about this, the Spirit said, "When I really show up, when My concentrated manifest presence hits the church, no one will be left in the pews. All will fall before Me." It has happened before. It happened, as I mentioned, when Christ was in the Garden of Gethsemane, and the Roman soldiers came to arrest Him. It happened in some of the incredible revival meetings in the 1800s and early 1900s. You can be certain that it will happen again as God answers the call of His people to come and fill the house once again with His glory.

Isaiah continued, "Then flew one of the seraphims unto me, having a live coal in his hand, which he had taken with the tongs from off the altar: And he laid it upon my mouth, and said, Lo, this hath touched thy lips; and thine iniquity is taken away, and thy sin purged" (Isa. 6:6–7). Notice that it was the lips of Isaiah, the righteous prophet, that the angel touched with the coal. Jesus explained how our words, uttered from our lips, reveal our defilement. He said, "There is nothing from without a man, that entering into him can defile him: but the things which come out of him, those are they that defile the man" (Mark 7:15). It is not what goes in that defiles, but it is what comes out—the words a person speaks. Why? Because what we speak springs forth from the depths of our hearts. If you really want to know someone or gauge their walk with God, just listen to them for awhile. They may be able to speak the right things for awhile, but eventually, what is in their heart will be spoken.

The coal from the altar not only cleansed Isaiah's lips; it also purged him. If you and I are to speak the revelation of God to this generation—if we are to bring forth the things of God—it is imperative that we become, and remain, holy vessels. How I long for ministers to get alone with God and get a word from God, rather than pouring over sermon books. The church desperately needs men and women to speak what God speaks to their hearts, not what they hear and read from other ministers. We have had enough regurgitated messages. Every time someone comes up with a new revelation or the rebirth of a long-lost doctrine, it becomes a fad. God has so much to share and so much for us to do that if we, as ministers and children of God, would just get alone with Him, He would release the revelation and insight we need for the hour.

I am fully convinced that we have not yet tapped into the fullness of what God wants to say or do in our midst. He is waiting for someone to get hungry enough and desperate enough for Him! I am not satisfied with the level of revelation and insight I have received from Him. I want more—and not just for the sake of having some new revelation to share. No, I want to speak things that truly flow from His heart! These are the words that will impact lives and bring men and women to Christ. Only His living words will cause a hunger to well up inside the listeners and birth a desire and urgency to draw closer to Him.

After Isaiah was cleansed with the coal from the altar, he heard the voice of the Lord saying "Whom shall I send, and who will go for us?" to which he responded, "Here am I; send me" (Isa. 6:8). God asked who would go, and Isaiah's immediate answer was, "Send me." The Father has never stopped asking that question. He reveals His heart to those who spend time alone with Him so that they can become aware of what God is doing and share it for the blessing of the church.

Isaiah did not run out from that "God encounter" and start telling everyone his vision. There is a great responsibility in walking close to God and hearing His voice. The Father not only tells you things about yourself, He also shares insights into His Word. These insights are given to minister to you and to others as well. Just as with Isaiah, God has shared insights with me about His Word so that I would be prepared to share it with a church or an individual as I ministered. Throughout church history, God has given fresh revelation to His people on many occasions. The truth that He reveals is not necessarily a new revelation or teaching; it is usually a rebirthing of a truth that the church has lost or discarded. For example, during the 1940s and 1950s there was an explosion of the gift of healing. In the 1980s there was an emergence of the teaching on spiritual warfare. During the early part of the twentieth century, the emphasis of the Holy Spirit was revelation of the baptism in the Spirit.

If you were to look back further in church history, you would see times when God created an awareness of holiness and other aspects of Christian living. Since the time of Christ, different men and women of God have been raised up to refocus the body of Christ's attention on God. Today God speaks to us in the same manner. Unfortunately, many of these insights have become no more than a fad when revealed by God's servants. Rather than running to God to get a fuller understanding of what they have heard from a minister, many instead try adding to the message their own thoughts or understandings. Thankfully, there are those who are obedient to what God speaks.

The river of His presence runs deep, and only a few seem to ever dive in to retrieve the deep things of God. My prayer for everyone who reads this book is that they will find the joy of unashamed, intimate encounters with the Father. He is waiting for you to cry out as Isaiah did, "Here am I; send me." I find great comfort and peace of mind when I read Isaiah. Praise God, Isaiah was not afraid to dive deeply into the presence of God. He gave us much insight as Christians into what we can anticipate in our walk with the Father.

It was Isaiah who wrote those comforting words as well: "Hast thou not known? hast thou not heard, that the everlasting God, the LORD, the Creator of the ends of the earth, fainteth not, neither is weary? there is no searching of his understanding. He giveth power to the faint; and to them that have no might he increaseth strength. Even the youths shall faint and be weary, and the young men shall utterly fall" (Isa. 40:28–30). Why should you worry about anything when you realize that God is always looking out for you? That is why Isaiah could prophesy with such boldness the judgments that he was instructed to speak. When you know God is in control, all hell can be breaking loose around you, but you will not care. When you find the joy of being in His presence, you will be like a little child being held by his parents. The child believes and acts as though everything is fine because Mommy or Daddy is holding him.

God spoke to Isaiah and said, "I am the Creator. I never grow weary. I never faint or tire." Therefore, God is able to give power to those who faint and to them with no might He increases their strength. The Hebrew text here indicates that God is continuously, non-stop, giving power and increasing strength. His strength is available to you now, in abundance. What we see as mere words when we read the Bible will become our substance and strength as we live them out! The cure for the many Christians and ministers who struggle with insecurity and mental breakdowns is found only in His presence. When will we learn to crawl up in our Father's lap and feel His heartbeat? When my daughter feels my arms wrapped around her, she has no fear. How much more should we feel safe in the arms of our heavenly Father? I encourage you to draw close to Him; He is waiting for you.

In Isaiah 40:31 we read, "But they that wait upon the Lord shall renew their strength; they shall mount up with wings as eagles; they shall run, and not be weary; and they shall walk, and not faint." I can only imagine the joy that Isaiah must have felt when God spoke these words to him. Can you imagine how big Isaiah's smile must have been? The country was going through turmoil; God's fierce judgment was about to fall. Because of this, many were growing weary and were giving up all hope. Then God said, "Hold on Isaiah; things don't look good, and yes, even the youth shall grow weary and faint. Many will lose hope and want to give up—but not those who wait upon the Lord." Sometimes as we read the Word, we only look at the surface; but look at it as it was spoken to Isaiah. The word for *wait* in the original Hebrew language means "to stay or rest in expectation." Some Christians think "to wait" means that you stand around and wait, hoping that something good will happen. Not so; the Father wants us to wait and rest in Him with expectancy that all will work out. God also spoke this wonderful promise to Isaiah: "For since the beginning of the world men have not heard, nor perceived by the ear, neither hath the eye seen, O God, beside thee, what he hath prepared for him that waiteth for him" (Isa. 64:4). It is that utter confidence that God is in control that renews our strength.

It does not stop there either, because God told Isaiah that not only would He renew their strength, they would also mount up with wings as eagles. Waiting upon the Lord implies getting alone with Him with the expectation that while we are waiting on Him we are resting in Him. This type of waiting is an active moving on our part; it is not being passive. As we wait, the Father renews our strength, and He begins to elevate us above our circumstances. To mount up with wings as eagles means to rise on high and to ascend above the clouds.

God could have stopped there, before telling Isaiah that we would ascend over the circumstances and problems, but He didn't. He promised we would "mount up with wings as eagles." God was calling Isaiah an eagle. The eagle has always been a symbol of superior freedom, protection, and strength. In fact, God told the Israelites, long before Isaiah's time, "Ye have seen what I did unto the Egyptians, and how I bare you on eagles' wings, and brought you unto myself" (Exod. 19:4). One reason we are to mount up is because God is bringing us to Himself! Eagles make their homes high up in the rocks; they do not feel at home on low ground. David once prayed, "From the end of the earth will I cry unto thee, when my heart is overwhelmed: lead me to the rock that is higher than I" (Ps. 61:2). If you're going to mount up as an eagle, then you are going to have to change your address. Quit making your dwelling place in the low ground. Allow the Spirit to move you higher in Christ, our Rock. Live above and not beneath!

Eagles also are finicky eaters. Unlike vultures, they will not eat anything that is dead or decayed. Eagles catch and eat fresh, live prey. The problems that many Christians face are the direct result of feasting on dead things. They are still living in the past, still holding onto their mistakes and shortcomings. Others are feasting on the spoiled food that the world offers, rather than feasting on the fresh bread of heaven. Jesus said,

> Verily, verily, I say unto you, except ye eat the flesh of the Son of man, and drink his blood, ye have no life in you. Whoso eateth my flesh, and drinketh my blood, hath eternal life; and I will raise him up at the last day. For my flesh is meat indeed, and my blood is drink indeed. He that eateth my flesh, and drinketh my blood, dwelleth in me, and I in him. As the living Father hath sent me, and I live by the Father: so he that eateth me, even he shall live by me. This is that bread which came down from heaven: not as your fathers did eat manna, and are dead: he that eateth of this bread shall live for ever.
>
> —JOHN 6:53–58

After Jesus made that statement, some of His followers came to him and said, "Jesus, we can't handle this so we're leaving." (See John 6:60.) If you are going to walk with God, you are going to have to be sustained by Him. This requires feasting on the fresh bread of heaven. Those followers who quit on Jesus that day were saying by their actions, "We'd rather eat the dead, dry, life-killing food that the world offers."

Are you living below what God intends for you? Have you been feasting on the garbage that the world has to offer? The packaging may look nice—even delicious—but the contents will destroy you! According to the apostle Paul, when you feast on the garbage of the world, you are eating with demons. Paul wrote, "Ye cannot drink the cup of the Lord, and the cup of devils: Ye cannot be partakers of the Lord's table, and the table of devils" (1 Cor. 10:21). You will either fly with the vultures, or you will soar like an eagle. It is this partaking of the bread of heaven and making your abode on the rock of your salvation that will cause the strength and rest of Isaiah 40:31 to become reality: You will run and not grow weary; you will walk and not faint.

Every step you take, every mile you run, no matter how difficult, God is right there with you. God spoke to Isaiah, "When you pass through the waters, I will be with you; and through the rivers, they shall not overflow you. When you walk through the fire, you shall not be burned, neither shall the flame scorch you" (Isa. 43:2, author's paraphrase). Some situations that we face in life may seem to be overwhelming to us just like a river with its strong currents. Yet in the midst of that trial, God is there to bring us through. When God says to walk with Him, He intends to be by your side every step of the way, the whole time. He will never fail you, so you need not worry about growing faint or weary or being overwhelmed. God says to you and me, "I will go before thee, and make the crooked places straight. I will break in pieces the gates of brass, and cut in sunder the bars of iron" (Isa. 45:2). For anything the enemy sends to stop and destroy us, God will remove the obstacles! Isaiah tells us, "The LORD will go before you, and the God of Israel will be your rear guard" (Isa. 52:12, author's paraphrase). And again through Isaiah, the Lord promises, "No weapon that is formed against thee shall prosper; and every tongue that shall rise against thee in judgment thou shalt condemn. This is the heritage of the servants of the LORD, and their righteousness is of me, saith the LORD" (Isa. 54:17).

As you long for Him and learn to enter into His presence, your place of security and dwelling will be made high up in the rocks like that of the eagle. You will learn to feast upon the life-giving, fresh bread of heaven. No matter what you face, you will feel the hand of God not only leading you, but also overshadowing you. God longs to draw you close to Himself. He desires intimate communion with His children. God spoke prophetically through Isaiah saying, "He that putteth his trust in me shall possess the land, and shall inherit my holy mountain" (Isa. 57:13). The holy mountain was God's dwelling place: "For thus saith the high and lofty One, that inhabits eternity, whose name is Holy; I dwell in the high and holy place" (v. 15). God wants us to dwell where He is. God also revealed this truth to the apostle Paul, who wrote: "And [God] hath raised us up together, and made us sit together in heavenly places in Christ Jesus" (Eph. 2:6).

As God draws us closer, He purges us more deeply. Because nothing unclean can draw close to Him, He purges us so that we can approach Him. God declared: "Depart ye, depart ye, go ye out from thence, touch no unclean thing; go ye out of the midst of her; be ye clean, that bear the vessels of the LORD" (Isa. 52:11). As carriers of His presence, we are to be clean. Only those set apart unto Him can be used mightily for Him. Drawing closer in intimate fellowship with God is not just for friendship with God and not only for our benefit; it is also for the benefit of others. Just as God revealed the scriptures to Isaiah by His Spirit that were to be a blessing to the world, so He wants to use us today to touch and impact the lives of others. For this purpose, He cleanses us and delivers us from our bondages. This is not to imply that what the Father reveals to us is infallible or on the same level as that spoken to the writers of the Word of God. What God spoke to them became the living Word, what He reveals to us is insight of the truths of that living Word.

The Holy Spirit recently taught me a truth about purity through reading the prophet Isaiah. In Isaiah 4, God uses the analogy of fire and burning as a means of purging and refining us: "When the Lord shall have washed away the filth of the daughters of Zion, and shall have purged the blood of Jerusalem from the midst thereof by the spirit of judgment, and by the spirit of burning" (Isa. 4:4). God wants us to be pure and holy so that we may approach Him. Yet, even after salvation, there is a process that we must go through as the Spirit works on us, changing us and cleaning us up. The prophet Malachi makes this process abundantly clear: "But who may abide the day of his coming? And who shall stand when he appeareth? For he is like a refiner's fire, and like fullers' soap...And he shall purify the sons of Levi, and purge them as gold and silver, that they may offer unto the Lord an offering in righteousness" (Mal. 3:2–3). The purpose of purity is that we will resemble Christ. Only in resembling Christ are we able to approach God. In other places, scripture teaches that we must be holy as He is holy. (See 1 Peter 1:16.)

In the Old Testament, before the high priest could go beyond the veil into the holy of holies, he had to closely examine his life. God made it very clear to the priests, as well as to everyone else, that for one to approach Him required purity and holiness. As we saw with Isaiah, the closer we get to God, the more we recognize the sin in our hearts. We begin to understand what things grieve Him. It is then that we are brought to the place where we grieve over the same things that grieve the Father.

As we discussed earlier, many people have tried to put on a man-made holiness: "If I only do this or that, God will accept me." Man-made efforts do not work; they only cause anguish, because our self-effort at purity will always fail. Even worse, our self-effort causes a judgmental or critical attitude as we begin believing that we are better, or more pious, than others. The truth of the matter is that only the Holy Spirit working in our lives can form the character of Christ in us. This refining work of the Holy Spirit takes a lifetime. Praise God that He sees us as being complete in Christ; He does not view us according to our incomplete beginnings.

Intimacy with God not only positions us to walk with God, it also allows Him the opportunity to speak to us individually as to the needs in our lives. As in human relationships, we are most comfortable hearing about our shortcomings from those with whom we have a close relationship. We receive their positive criticism because of the closeness of the relationship we share. It is similar in our relationship with the Father. He is careful to reveal things to us at the time that we are not only ready to receive it, but when we are also willing to do what is necessary to correct it.

When I pastored full time, I did not use my time in the pulpit to beat the people over the head. Rather, I simply taught the Word, knowing that the closer the people got to the Father's heart, the more change could take place in their lives. The Bible characterizes God as light, in whom there is no darkness. (See 1 John 1:5.) The closer we draw to that light, the more the darkness in our hearts is revealed so it can be dealt with. Isaiah tells us that first there must be a purging fire. He wrote, "And the LORD will create upon every dwelling place of Mount Zion, and upon her assemblies, a cloud and smoke by day, and the shining of a flaming fire by night: for upon all the glory shall be a defence. And there shall be a tabernacle for a shadow in the daytime from the heat, and for a place of refuge, and for a covert from storm and from rain" (Isa. 4:5–6). Before God's glory, which is His manifest presence, will cover us and be evident in our lives, we must go through the purging process.

The purpose of this purging is to make us—each of us—a burning bush, a minister of fire. (See Hebrews 1:7.) The body of Christ should be ablaze with the fire of God, yet many have been content to only offer a smoldering heat of a passion long since passed away. But I have a word for the church of Jesus Christ: God is reigniting a passion for Him in a remnant of people who are hungry for intimacy with Him. This remnant will not be satisfied with man-made, flesh-inspired preaching and mechanical worship expressions. This remnant longs and thirsts for God to take His rightful place as the Head of their church and their lives. They are hungry. No, they are desperate for the holy fire of His presence to set them ablaze. In the last days the church is going to see a new breed of Christians and ministers come on the scene. When they speak, it will be the Father's heartbeat the hearers will sense.

Will you be one of them? How hungry for Him are you? Isaiah was never the same after catching a glimpse of God on His throne. Like those before and after him, this encounter resulted in a desire to draw closer to the Father. The flesh shrinks back, but our spirits cry out for another touch. Oh, that I might feel His breath upon my cheek! How I long to feel His heartbeat, to feel His hand on me, to hear the whisper of His voice! Are you hungry for Him? Do you desire Him above all others? Like Isaiah, let Him hear us cry out, "Here am I. Send me!" I want to see more than His throne; I want to see Him. How about you?

*"For therefore
came I forth…"*
—MARK 1:38

CHAPTER 10

JESUS

Purposeful Pursuit

The primary reason Christ invaded our earthly realm was to bring us back into right relationship with God, the Father. From the time He first created Adam, until the time He sent Christ, God longed for intimate communion with His most precious creation, mankind; therefore, the main reason Christ came was to restore us to that relationship. Few had found their way back to Him under the demands of the law. Something had to be done; so, in the plan of God, Christ came to fix what Adam had messed up. Scripture refers to Christ as the last Adam: "So it is written, 'The first man, Adam, was made a living soul.' The last Adam became a life-giving spirit. The first man is of the earth, earthy; the second man is from heaven" (1 Cor. 15:45, 47, author's paraphrase).

The first Adam opened a door of pain and heartache. Even worse, he brought upon himself and the whole human race death and separation from God. What Christ did for us was to open an avenue to the Father's heart that would be available to all. Christ came to undo all that the enemy had done

thousands of years earlier by deception in the Garden of
Eden. After the Fall of mankind into disobedience to God,
only a select group or nation was permitted to walk in
covenant relationship with Him. This was not God's original
plan, but it became a necessary part of the plan of redemp-
tion after the Fall. Even with the privilege of the covenant
relationship with God, very few of His beloved Israelites
sought Him. Gentiles were left out unless they converted to
be a part of the nation of Israel.

Jesus brought the restoration of what God intended in the
very beginning. Now all races can have intimate communion and friendship with the Father! I am so thankful that
God came in the form of a Man, Jesus Christ, to remove
these barriers of separation, so hungry people like you and
me could pursue God. Jesus said, "He that hath seen me
hath seen the Father" (John 14:9). Christ, who was with the
Father from the foundation of the world, knew above all
others the way to the Father's heart. The intimacy that
hungry people sought and the manifest presence of God for
which they longed was made available through the life,
death and resurrection of Christ. Jesus said, "No man
cometh unto the Father, but by me" (John 14:6). John, one
of Christ's disciples, wrote: "No man hath seen God at any
time: the only begotten Son, which is in the bosom of the
Father, he hath declared him" (John 1:18). Only Christ can
declare the Father to us in all of His glory.

Jesus did not come just to remove the barriers caused by
sin and to save us. He came to reveal to us the Father's heart
and to show us the way to His heart. Christ not only fulfilled
the law through His death and resurrection, becoming "the
Way" to the Father; He also gave us a pattern to follow in
the way He walked and lived before the Father. Mark wrote,
"And in the morning, rising up a great while before day, he
went out, and departed into a solitary place, and there
prayed" (Mark 1:35). Jesus never let anything interfere with
His intimate communion with the Father. He not only prac-
ticed being alone with the Father, but He also taught His

disciples to do the same. He admonished them to get alone with God and pray. (See Matthew 6:6.) People say that they can pray as they drive to work or when they are doing the dishes. That is true, but an intimate communion with Him requires being alone and undistracted. I can communicate with my wife on a cell phone driving down the road or while watching television, but does she really have my full, undivided attention? No! When you must be aware of other drivers around you, or you are involved in a movie plot, your attention is divided. When my wife and I spend an evening in intimate communion and fellowship, she expects my full attention so I can give her my whole self. The Father expects nothing less from us; that is what Jesus showed and taught us. He told the Samaritan woman at the well, "But the hour cometh, and now is, when the true worshippers shall worship the Father in spirit and in truth: for the Father seeketh such to worship him" (John 4:23). One of the root meanings of the Greek word translated *worship* means "to kiss and adore." The word translated *spirit* means "the entire being." Though we should commune with the Father all day long, practicing His presence through singing and talking to Him, we also need times of aloneness with Him. I would not allow anyone else or any distractions to steal my attention while I am alone with my wife; she would not permit it. If I did, it would give her the impression that she is not worth my undivided attention. God feels the same way.

God said of Israel, "And I will visit upon her the days of Baalim, wherein she burned incense to them, and she decked herself with her earrings and her jewels, and she went after her lovers, and forgot me, saith the LORD" (Hos. 2:13). God was upset and grieved that Israel would want anyone else over Him, yet, how many of us have done the same thing? God wants some time alone with us, but we have brought our other lovers along! Oh, we say that we do not have other lovers, but when our possessions come before Him, when our family comes before Him, when our blessings come before him, we are no better than a harlot. That is exactly what God called Israel. When we put even our ministry before Him, as the Pharisees did, we have cheated on Him. I have met pastors who spend more time building their "ministry kingdom" than they do building their relationship with God. Please hear my warning, ministers; the very things that will sustain you are being ignored. If you are not careful, you will fall. If Jesus saw the necessity of intimate communion with the Father, how much more should we? Of course, Jesus came from the Father's bosom; He knew the Father's heartbeat. Perhaps that is why more do not seek Him; they have never felt His heartbeat. When you have really been in His presence, you will want to go there again!

Jesus' ministry and life models for us the type of relationship we should strive and long for. On a number of occasions, when asked where His authority came from, Jesus replied, "I can of mine own self do nothing: as I hear, I judge: and my judgment is just; because I seek not mine own will, but the will of the Father which hath sent me" (John 10:4). In other words, He said He spoke only the things that He heard from His Father. That is the place the Father wants each of His children to be, the place of hearing from Him with clarity. Jesus said, "And when he putteth forth his own sheep, he goeth before them, and the sheep follow him: for they know his voice" (John 10:4). How many of us have positioned ourselves to hear from Him? Would we recognize Him if He spoke? A friend of mine confided in me the other day, "Jesse, some days, when I read the Bible, the things God is speaking to me seem to leap off the page. At other times, I may go days without any new understanding." I explained to him that, especially as a new Christian, the primary avenue of hearing from God is through the Scriptures. We learn to know Him and discern His voice by reading the Word. For that reason, what God has to share with us may take a few days to sink into our spirits. Sometimes it takes awhile before the Holy Spirit can drive the Word home, so to speak. Eventually, we will become more familiar with His voice, and the Spirit will start to give us more spiritual understanding. It may come from a scripture or a story in the Word. It may be a message that we heard recently from another minister. Perhaps it will just be the Father whispering His love to us. It has the same effect as when we read the Word and it seems to leap off the page. As I explained to my friend, these spiritual impressions are the Lord speaking to us. When we learn to recognize that impression on our spirit (as long as it agrees with the written Word), we will not go days without hearing from the Father. Soon we will learn to hear the Father speaking to us every day in some fashion, because He longs to commune with us. If you struggle to hear Him, read the Word, not as just another book, but as His letter to you. Become familiar with His ways as revealed in His Word. And He will develop in you, by His Spirit, a hearing ear.

Jesus said many times, "Blessed are they who hear" (Luke 11:28; Matt. 13:16; Rev. 1:3). Jesus not only heard His Father's voice, but He also walked in obedience to the Father. God is so awesome! As a loving Father, He desires only the best for His children. You and I have the privilege of not only speaking to the Father, but also hearing Him speak back. Some people may say, "God doesn't speak to us today." That is false. He does speak to us today, and although I have never heard an audible voice, I have learned to know that inner still small voice. The closer I draw to God, the more sensitive I become to His voice.

I cannot stress enough the importance of learning to know the voice of God. Our minds and spirits are bombarded with many different voices. There is the voice of our own reasoning and there is the voice of the enemy. There are the voices of our friends, and, of course, the voice of our own thoughts and desires. Learning to navigate through those voices and to concentrate only on hearing the voice of the Lord can take time. Please do not struggle with this process. People worry that they will not hear His voice or that they will become confused trying to figure out if what they hear is really God's voice. A word of wisdom here: His voice is always peaceful, and it will never violate what He has already revealed to us in the written Word, the Bible.

Some people, ministers included, think that every thought that jumps into their minds is from God, regardless of how silly the thought may be. God will never reveal or speak something to us that does not line up with what He has already revealed in His Word. I teach people that if what they feel God has shown them is not directly mentioned in the Word, then the next step is to see if what they are doing or what they have been told violates the overall message or principles of the Word. I can honestly say that as I have drawn closer to Him, not only have I been hearing the Holy Spirit more frequently, but I am also hearing with greater clarity. This is due, in part, to my wanting to hear Him, so I am listening more intently. The times that Christ spent alone in prayer were spent talking and listening to the Father. God has much to share with you, but if you rush through your times of being alone with Him and if you do not take the time to be still and silent, you will always struggle in hearing His voice and knowing His will. The Word of God declares: "Be still, and know that I am God" (Ps. 46:10). If, while communing with my wife, I never stopped talking to let her speak, I would never know what was on her mind. If you want to know what the Father has to say, give Him an opportunity to speak to you.

As you study the life of Christ, it becomes evident that He was totally committed to obeying the Father in all things. Some may say this was because Jesus was the Son of God; He would, of course, be sold out to the Father. But just as Christ was God come in the flesh, so He was also a Man. He had to learn things much the same way we do. We know that He was tempted, yet He did not succumb to those temptations. As a Spirit-filled Man, He learned to walk with God and developed a relationship the same way you and I must develop our relationship with Him. Christ came to show us the way, and I am going to follow Him and pursue the Father as Jesus pursued Him. What an awesome Savior Christ is!

As our Savior, Lord and lover, He longs for only the best and wants you and me to enjoy the closeness with Him and the Father that He enjoys. Jesus said, "That they all may be one; as thou, Father, art in me, and I in thee, that they also may be one in us: that the world may believe that thou hast sent me" (John 17:21). Christ was one with the Father in everything He did as a Man—in words, in thoughts and in deeds. As we read earlier, Christ was in the Father's bosom. The same place the Father has placed us, in His bosom, is the place where we can feel and hear His heartbeat.

Our pursuit of Christ and the Father should be as intense as Christ's pursuit of the Father. We come to understand that intensity when we read the Gospels and look at the lives of those who followed Christ. However, I want to focus our attention now only on the life of Christ as He lived in pursuit of the Father. After all, Christ came to restore that garden relationship with us that the first Adam let slip away. When you study the life of Christ, you begin to understand that His attitude, His actions, and everything about Him reflected the heart of the Father.

We can catch a glimpse of something else Christ was sent to restore in us by studying an encounter He had with a Samaritan woman at a well. (See John 4.) During their brief conversation, He revealed something of the Father's heart that had been misunderstood. Christ used that encounter to bring to light the Father's desire for intimate communion, for true worship—not worship as we sometimes define it in the singing of a song and lifting of our hands toward heaven. These are expressions of worship, but they do not define true worship according to God's definition. This woman asked Jesus where the correct place of worship was, since their fathers worshiped on a mountain and others said Jerusalem was the place to worship. Jesus discounted her question and gave us the definition of true worship in His response: "But the hour cometh, and now is, when the true worshippers shall worship the Father in spirit and in truth: for the Father seeketh such to worship him. God is a Spirit:

and they that worship him must worship him in spirit and in truth" (John 4:23–24).

The kind of worship Jesus is speaking about here is that which flows from our innermost being. It is the result of giving our all to God as the central force of our lives. We were created for fellowship and communion with God. Worship is the natural outflow of that intimate relationship with Him. Intimacy births worship, and worship births intimacy. Jesus revealed that where we worship is not as important as how we worship Him. The Father is not that concerned with where we are, but He is seeking worshipers who will wholeheartedly worship Him. In order to touch His heart, we must give Him our *whole* heart.

The Holy Spirit told me the other day while I was writing this chapter, "Sin gains a foothold and creates a stronghold where there is no true worship." The apostle Paul addresses the issue of misplaced worship, saying that some people "worshipped and served the creature more than the Creator, who is blessed forever" (Rom. 1:25). He then describes the tragic result of this false worship. (See Romans 1:26–31.) Worship is naturally directed to that which has the central place in our lives. If our focus is on ourselves, we will only do those things that please us. We see that in the verses following Paul's statement about worshiping the creation over God. This illustrates that true worship is a lifestyle, not just an expression or form, as we often mistakenly think in the church. Many people have the idea that worship is going to church, hearing a song and singing. They think that they are worshiping when they participate in these worship expressions. A look at their lifestyle shows they do not really worship in spirit and truth, yet they will tell you that they worship God. This is because our idea of worship is not the same as God's. He longs for our entire heart, not just a song. When worship is a lifestyle born out of relationship, everything we do is worship unto Him. Our hearts are surrendered to His will in all of life. When worship is a lifestyle, the songs we sing, the dances we do, even our uplifted hands all become cxpressions of our worship to Him. God is restoring true worship as Christ taught the Samaritan woman. True worship is an obedient, loving response to God in spirit and in truth.

Worship without relationship is just dead emotionalism; it is going through the motions just because someone on the platform says to lift your hands and follow them as they lead another song. In response to these lifeless worship expressions, Jesus said, "This people draweth nigh unto me with their mouth, and honoureth me with their lips; but their heart is far from me. But in vain they do worship me, teaching for doctrines the commandments of men" (Matt. 15:8–9). The question we are faced with is, "What or who is central in my life? Am I a worshiper in the definition of what Christ had in mind, or am I just going through the motions because I am in church?" You see, we can only become effective worshipers corporately as a body according to who we are individually as we live our lives before God. Unfortunately, many times we bring so much junk to church with us that it takes an hour of prodding and singing just to get everyone to a place of unified worship. No wonder pastors have to tug and plead for everyone to be participants rather than spectators on Sunday morning.

It is no wonder our nation does not experience a move of God as He desires—when we are central in our lives and He is not. In that situation we really do not worship Him at all. I thank God that He is changing our pitiful condition. More and more people are starting to get a hunger for the things of God and are forsaking their selfish pursuits. God is not only calling us to intimate communion, but also to wholehearted worship that flows from our innermost being. Expressing that worship involves uttering words and singing songs of intimate desire and longing for Him. Get ready for the radicals who are coming on the scene, desiring only to worship God in spirit and truth!

I realize that there are some people, as the result of their past, who do not believe God would accept their worship or pursuit of Him. Let me encourage you that God sees you through the eyes of Christ once you have accepted Him as Savior and followed Him in baptism. When Christ came up out of the water after His baptism, the voice of the Father thundered from heaven, "This is my beloved son, in whom I am well pleased!" (Matt. 17:5). The Father feels the same way toward you and me; He is well pleased when we are walking with Him. One reason some people have a hard time approaching the Father and accepting His love is because of the relationship they had with their earthly fathers. Their perception of their earthly fathers affects their perception of their heavenly Father. Please hear me: your heavenly Father is well pleased with you; nothing you do will ever change His love toward you. Although we may do things that grieve Him or break His heart, He will always love us with a deep, consuming love.

A few years ago I counseled a young couple, and the wife could not seem to draw close to God. No matter how much they came to church or prayed, she just could not seem to receive the love of God. While at their home counseling them, the Lord spoke to me and said, "Tell her to quit comparing Me to her earthly father." When I said that to this young lady, she looked at me blankly and said, "What?" I repeated myself, "The Lord said to quit comparing Him to your earthly father." She immediately began to cry. She had grown up with a father who was very strict, which had given her a distorted view of Father God. After that counseling experience, I began to understand why some Christians struggle to receive the love of God. Unfortunately, some people reject His love because of their past. Christ represents the heart of the Father. In fact, to see Christ in His tender compassion and healing power is to see the Father; to hear Christ is to hear the Father. One cannot look at Christ without seeing the intensity of the Father's love. Christ never condemned anyone. Those He did rebuke were the religious crowd who rejected Him. He rebuked them because of the distorted view they held of Him. Regardless of your past or current relationship with your earthly father, know that your heavenly Father will never abuse you. He will never take advantage of you. He will never leave you. He only desires good for you. He loves you with an everlasting love. Do not let your past or your present circumstances hinder you from experiencing the closeness He longs to have with you.

Something else we learn from Christ is the zeal He had for the things of God. John gave one of the most vivid accounts of this zeal. He tells us that Jesus went into the temple one day and drove out those who were selling and buying merchandise. According to the scriptures, the temple was to be a place of prayer. (See Isaiah 56:7.) The actual word Jesus used for *prayer* means "worship." Jesus declared, "It is written, My house is the house of prayer: but ye have made it a den of thieves" (Luke 19:46). The people were being attracted to the house of God not because God was there, but because of what was being promoted, the things being sold. Jesus saw the situation, and a holy anger rose up within Him. I believe the reason He called them thieves is because they were stealing God's time. Rather than pointing the people to Him, they had their attention for the sake of monetary gain. Perhaps the reason so few people get anything from our services is because they are not attracted to our church by God, but by what we are selling and offering. If we promote our music program or our speaker over Him, then we shouldn't expect people to receive the life of God; we're only stealing His time. The closer you draw to His heart, the more sensitive you become to the things of God. You will find yourself more and more disappointed at things happening in the church that are not right. John said of Jesus, "And his disciples remembered that it was written, The zeal of thine house hath eaten me up" (John 2:17).

My wife came home the other day and said her friend came to work upset about what she had witnessed Sunday morning at her church. She said while the minister was pouring his heart out in the message, he went about fifteen minutes past his normal closing time. Some people just got up and walked out, which visibly upset the pastor. When my wife told me about the incident, it broke my heart. A holy indignation rose up within me. Are we so insensitive that we will not even allow God to speak to us unless it is within the time allotted? Who are we to even consider such a thing? Some may disagree with me, but I believe those who refuse to give God His time will not go to heaven. This is the pattern of the Pharisees of Jesus' day. Every time Christ performed a miracle, they condemned and rejected Him because He did not conform to their religious law and rituals. Christ saved His harshest rebukes for the Pharisees. He told them that they made the Word of God of no effect by their traditions. My heart breaks to see Christians come to church with the attitude that they are doing God a favor by giving Him an hour on Sunday. Jesus looked at the sales people in the temple hawking their goods, and it grieved and angered Him. The place that should have been filled with seekers was filled with sellers! Rather than seeking God for their nation, they were peddling their wares. Are we much different today if we come to church to be entertained rather than to hear His heartbeat? And then, satisfied that we have done our Christian duty, we go home to live our lives without seeking Him further.

The reason that the majority—yes, the majority—of our churches are dead, dry and barren like a desert is because there is no hunger in the pulpit or in the pew. Few ministers challenge their people to draw closer to Him. We offer a watered-down gospel and preach an "anything goes, it's all right" message that requires no commitment yet promises the world to those who will receive it. Ministers proclaim that if you give, you will receive their special blessing, which is only flowing through their ministry or church. Because of this polluted gospel, our churches are filled with people who have no hunger for God, no real spiritual life. Without real biblical substance, these people will not finish the race. No wonder the church in America has lost members and has not had any significant growth for more than ten years while false religions are booming with growth. People are coming seeking life, and all we can offer is a good song and dance. We make certain to thank them for visiting us and give them a reception after the service, complete with coffee and donuts! Yet rarely do they come back, because most churches do not offer anything different than what they can find elsewhere—a temporary band-aid for their heartache.

Not every church is like that, of course; there are some dynamic churches where hungry people gather to worship the Father in spirit and in truth. In such churches you will find people who love others and accept them with open arms. I thank God that I attend a vibrant church that offers more than just shallow ritual. Pastors come from all over the country and even from different parts of the world to enjoy a few services with us during our pastors' conferences. It is not because we are special; it is because we allow the Holy Spirit to flow as He desires. We have learned to step out of the way and let Him have His way. Pastors and others are gloriously restored, renewed, rejuvenated and revived in His presence. It is God's presence that draws them to come to our small town to gather with our 400-plus people. We have no agenda other than to seek after Him and to hear a word from God. Our pastor continually tells us, "It is not about us; it is all about Him." This is the message of Christ! He declared that He came to reveal the Father to us and that those who had seen Him had seen the Father. (See John 14:9.) In our church we have been privileged to have some of God's choicest servants come to minister, but they do not attempt to impress God or us; they are only impressed *with* Him. That is what Christ was teaching people. Do not do things to impress others or yourself. Everything we do should be to one day hear Him say, "Well done, thou good and faithful servant" (Matt. 25:21).

Christ was angry at what He observed in the temple and with the religious leaders of His day. Some things in the church will break our hearts, too. Let us hold up Christ as our standard in our pursuit of the Father's heart. His zeal, His love, His longing to be with the Father, can and should be our standard. Are you still hungry for only Him? I know the Father is longing for you to draw closer and to get to know Him more intimately. Will you take that next step? Will you move beyond the veil into His awesome presence where there is only you and Him? The Father is waiting to overwhelm you with His love. You only need to walk toward Him.

*"Now there was leaning
on Jesus' bosom one of his disciples,
whom Jesus loved."*

—JOHN 13:23

CHAPTER 11

JOHN

Feeling His Heartbeat

John was no doubt greatly affected by Jesus' earthly ministry. Though there were many people who followed Christ, there was within that large group of people a group of twelve whom He had chosen to be part of His core group of disciples. And among those twelve there were three who seemed to spend more time with Him: Peter, James, and John. They even had the privilege of being with Him on the mountain during the solemn event of His transfiguration. (See Matthew 17:2.) And, among those three, one was especially close to Him—the person known as "the disciple whom Jesus loved." John held that precious title. As we look at John's life, it is no wonder why Jesus loved him so much. John had an overwhelming, consuming love for Christ.

There is much we can glean from John's life of love for Christ. In the book authored by him that bears his name, we find an interesting account of what is known as the Lord's Supper. (See John 13.) This chapter gives us great insight into John's relationship with Christ. Unaware of how few short hours Christ had left with them before He would give His life for the sins of the world, the disciples were relaxing and enjoying the Passover meal, sitting around the table fellowshiping with each other. Reading the chapter, we catch a glimpse of John's intimate relationship with Christ: "Now there was leaning on Jesus' bosom one of his disciples, whom Jesus loved" (John 13:23). Did Jesus love all of the disciples? Yes, of course. But as we have come to understand, there are degrees of intimacy in our relationships. Some, therefore, are closer to Him than others. John had a special place in Jesus' heart. Throughout the book of John, John is referenced with the title, "the disciple whom Jesus loved."

I believe that every time they ate together, John would lean against Jesus. Anytime my wife or I go someplace with our kids, one of them will yell out, "I get the front seat!" That one then gets to ride in the front on the way to where we're going, and the other has to wait until the trip home. I can imagine that when Jesus advised the disciples they would be dining together, John would yell out, "I get the seat next to Jesus!"

Men may find this hard to comprehend because many of us cannot remember the last time we "leaned against" another man, in openly affectionate relationship. If we can, it was probably with our own earthly fathers when we were very young. While women usually have no problem hugging each other or lounging around together, men typically limit their interaction to a pat on the back or a handshake. Therefore, I remind men that Christ said it is necessary to approach the kingdom of God as a little child. As a child of God, I long for nothing more than to crawl up in my Daddy's lap and lay my head on His chest. John was not afraid to lay his head against Christ's bosom. In that childlike relationship, Christ referred to John as the one whom He loved. I will be honest; I am jealous of John. What an incredible relationship he must have had with Christ! I told the Lord one day while walking, "Father, I know I'll be able to touch you and hug you in heaven, but I can't wait until then. I want to touch you now!" Although some will say that I am asking for the impossible, I believe that I will touch Him. I believe that it is possible and that it will happen. I know we walk by faith and not by sight or feelings, and I do not live on experience only but by the Word; but from what I have studied in the lives of God's people, I believe that it is possible to get so close to Him that we can feel His heartbeat.

John not only heard the heartbeat of Jesus through His words; he also felt His heartbeat. There is a difference. Many people can hear His heart expressed, but you have to touch Him in order to feel His heartbeat! To feel His heartbeat requires a closeness that few people pursue or attain to. There are many people today who hear God's heartbeat as a result of others touching Him and then sharing what they heard from Him. Once while ministering I told our church that each time we hear our pastor or a guest minister, we are hearing God's heart, thus His heartbeat. As wonderful as that may be, I do not want just to hear His heart; I want to feel His heartbeat by touching Him myself. For one to hear God's heart firsthand, he must be close to Him. Those who hear His heartbeat secondhand, by someone sharing God's heart with them, do not have to be close at all. You can walk up to a sinner on the street and share God's heart with them, but if they are to hear God's heart for themselves, it requires that they surrender their lives and begin a pursuit of God.

At this supper, Jesus told His disciples that one would betray Him. The disciples reacted to Jesus' statement and wanted to know who could do that. John gives this account: "Simon Peter therefore beckoned to him, that he should ask [Jesus] who it should be of whom He spake" (John 13:24). Peter motioned to John, who was leaning on Jesus, to ask the Lord who was to betray Him. Peter undoubtedly asked John to ask Jesus because John was the closest to Him at the table and because everyone recognized the closeness of his relationship with Christ. John must have whispered his question into Christ's ear; no doubt Christ whispered the answer into John's ear. This seems probable because, when

Judas ran out from the dinner, no one seemed to know where he was going, nor did they know why Judas left.

People are drawn to those who hear God's heartbeat. They are the ones who know what is on the Father's mind. God wants each of us to know His mind and heart—His purposes in the earth. The apostle Paul reveals this fact when he writes: "For this cause we also, since the day we heard it, do not cease to pray for you, and to desire that ye might be filled with the knowledge of his will in all wisdom and spiritual understanding; That ye might walk worthy of the Lord unto all pleasing, being fruitful in every good work, and increasing in the knowledge of God" (Col. 1:9–10). The apostle Paul expressed God's desire for us to increase in our understanding of God in both wisdom and spiritual understanding. Paul was not just speaking about head knowledge, which involves knowing *about* God. He was speaking of heart knowledge, which involves knowing Him intimately. To receive spiritual understanding requires closeness with the Father. In our human relationships, we understand that if you want to get to know someone, you have to hang out where they do. This is so beautifully modeled in the life of Christ when, as a Boy of twelve years, He was found in the temple asking questions of the teachers. Because of John's closeness to Christ, the other disciples asked him to question Jesus about things that they could not or would not ask themselves.

It is important to note how John addresses Jesus on this occasion: "He then lying on Jesus' breast saith unto him, Lord, who is it?" (John 13:25). John acknowledges Jesus as Lord. No matter how close we get to Him, He will always be Lord. Never take that for granted. Although we are heirs of God, joint heirs with Christ and, yes, friends also, He is and always will be our Savior and our Lord. Sometimes we do not esteem highly that which is familiar to us. Just as a church may be accustomed to the Spirit moving mightily during every service and come to expect it, so they may even lose their sense of awe of what the Spirit is doing. The way some ministers strut across the stage and flaunt the anointing while on the platform, you might think that they can do anything. Oh, we need to be careful that our closeness with God does not cause us to lose our reverence for His lordship. We must guard our holy, reverential fear of Him!

Another interesting event we see in John's life happened shortly after Christ's resurrection from the dead. The disciples had gone fishing; Jesus was on the beach cooking their breakfast. Jesus called out to them and asked if they had caught anything. Of the disciples who were fishing, John was the first to recognize the Lord in His glorified body: "Therefore that disciple whom Jesus loved saith unto Peter, It is the Lord" (John 21:7). Those who spend time in His presence recognize when He is near. There was something about the form of that Man on the beach; about His voice. He wasn't recognizable to the others, but John had that inner knowing—it was the Lord! It is possible to become so familiar with Christ in the secret place that you know immediately when He is near. There are times while I am praying that I know He has stepped into the room. During those times, I begin to weep as I bow to His lordship. Not long ago after an exceptional church service, my wife and I were lying in bed talking about what the Lord had done that evening. Suddenly, He came in; we were both aware of His presence at the moment He arrived. My wife whispered to me, "What if He visibly appears?" I replied, "I think I'd die!"

That may sound strange, especially since I have expressed my desire to see Him; however, at that moment, sensing the awe of His wonderful presence, I do not know what I would have done if He had shown Himself visibly. There are those who say there is no need for Him to show up visibly; therefore, He will not. My reply to them is, "Just tell that to John, who saw Christ after His resurrection. Tell that to the others who saw Him after His resurrection. Tell that to Paul, who saw the Lord on a number of occasions." There is nothing in the Word of God that implies differently. In fact, John records these words of Christ: "He that hath my commandments, and keepeth them, he it is that loveth me: and he that loveth me shall be loved of my Father, and I will love him, and will manifest myself to him" (John 14:21). He said that He would manifest Himself—appear, show up, and exhibit Himself—to the person who loves Him; therefore, I choose to accept nothing less than what He has promised to do!

After Jesus finished eating with the disciples, He asked Peter to walk with Him. While they walked and talked, Jesus spoke to Peter about the type of death Peter would experience. The scripture records the scene that follows: "Then Peter, turning about, seeth the disciple whom Jesus loved following; which also leaned on his breast at supper, and said, Lord, which is he that betrayeth thee? Peter seeing him saith to Jesus, Lord, and what shall this man do?" (John 21:20–21). John had been following Peter and Jesus while they walked along the seashore. I believe that John followed because he longed to be near the heart of God. Here was the one whose heartbeat John had felt, and John just could not stay away from Him. I can only imagine what Christ was feeling at that moment to see John following Him. What a passionate pursuit was evident in John! Christ had so impacted him during those last three and one-half years that he did not want to be apart from Him! John brings to my mind the psalmist's cry: "As the hart panteth after the water brooks, so panteth my soul after thee, O God" (Ps. 42:1). There are times when I have to run out the door for a quick trip to the store, and one of my children will say, "Wait, Dad, I want to come with you." I do not care if I have to wait another ten minutes while they get ready, it is hard to say no when I hear the love in their voice. I believe that Jesus would have done anything for John that day. Such was His love and desire toward John.

Similarly, Christ loves to turn around and see us in hot pursuit of Him. My spiritual forefathers will not outdo me. John's pursuit of Jesus never diminished with age. Many years later, while in his nineties, John was sent to a rocky, lonely place called Patmos. From the opening verses of the book of Revelation, we are given the impression that John's desire and love for God was still all-consuming. We are told that while he was communing with the Lord in the Spirit, "he heard a great voice, as of a trumpet" (Rev. 1:10). John saw Jesus that day and wrote, "And when I saw him, I fell at his feet as dead. And he laid his right hand upon me, saying unto me, Fear not; I am the first and the last" (Rev. 1:17). This was not just another dream or vision John was experiencing; it was so real that John actually felt the Lord touch him.

We need to realize that the spiritual realm is what is real. We call the things in our natural dimension "reality" because we can see them, taste them, hear them, and touch them. However, what we can see, taste, hear, and touch is only a copy of what has already been created in the spiritual realm. Heaven is filled with trees and animals, and was prior to the creation. The spiritual realm is more real than the physical. To take John's experience lightly because he was in the Spirit is to miss the reality of it. What we can now experience with our senses will one day fade away to be replaced with a new heaven and new earth in an entirely different dimension, the unseen spiritual dimension. Certainly it will not be unseen for long, for the Lord is coming back to clothe us with our spiritual bodies. (See 1 Corinthians 15:54.)

It is wonderful to meet people who have walked with God for years and whose love for Him is growing continually more intense. Their experience should be the norm. Our relationship with God should intensify just as two people are more in love after many years of marriage than they were when they first married. Ask yourself: "Am I more in love with Him now than when I was first saved? Is my desire and hunger for God stronger today than yesterday?" One thing I always pray is for the Holy Spirit to help me seek after God with my whole heart, not just with my lips. If we pursue God with anything less than our whole heart, that weak desire will soon diminish and disappear. Even hot coals will eventually cool off unless they are continually stirred up and fed.

When Christ was born, Anna, the prophetess, was eagerly awaiting His birth. For years she had remained faithful to

God, living a life of fasting and prayer in the temple of God.
(See Luke 2:36–37.) She held on to the memory of something
God had whispered to her years earlier. God had told her that
she would see the Messiah before her death. What would
cause a person to offer such devoted service, to continue
daily in the temple? Nothing short of an exciting and vibrant
relationship with the Father! If our seeking after the Father
is done out of duty, it will die; but when it is done from a
truly hungry heart, it will be the most exciting journey we
will ever take!

John, nearing the end of his life, was exiled on the island
of Patmos, yet it did not lessen His relationship with the
Lord. During that time he received one of the greatest revelations of the End Times. This shows us that, regardless of
our suffering, we can continue to have closeness with God
that propels us forward in Him. It was said of Jesus, "…who
for the joy that was set before him endured the cross, despising the shame, and is set down at the right hand of the throne
of God" (Heb. 12:2). When you are lost in His presence, your
painful circumstances will not have much effect because of
the deep, reassuring peace that is yours as you cuddle in the
Father's lap. How can you be concerned with things around
you when you are having such a good time with the Father?
Children at play are not aware of time. They do not worry
whether the bills are paid or whether groceries are in the
cupboard. We need to become like children and return to
that place of total abandonment. John suffered many things
prior to his banishment to Patmos, yet all of that faded in the
glorious presence of his Lord. Can you imagine the joy that
must have flooded John upon seeing Christ? Though we
have no record of any of John's experiences between his walk
on the beach and this revelation on Patmos, I know that John
maintained a closeness with Christ.

History tells us that John was eventually released from
Patmos and went on to serve as pastor of the church at
Ephesus. Can you imagine what his sermons must have been
like? I enjoy listening to people who have a close walk with

God. When they speak, it is as if God Himself is speaking. Anyone can open up the Bible, pick a subject, research it, and share the information with the audience; but when you come from His presence with a word from Him, your message is more than mere words—it is God-breathed! It is life-giving! Speaking of Jesus' message, Matthew wrote, "For he taught them as one having authority, and not as the scribes" (Matt. 7:29).

John spent a lifetime in passionate pursuit of his Lord. He never forgot what it felt like to hear His heartbeat. Are you hungry for Him? There awaits a closeness with the Father for you. Draw close to Him now. Cry out to Him. Let Him know that you long to feel His heartbeat. I will tell you a secret: His heart beats passionately for you. The Father longs to wrap His arms around you and draw you close to Him. Go ahead, crawl up into your heavenly Father's lap and lay your head upon His chest. Do you feel His heartbeat?

*"But when it pleased God,
who separated me..."*
—GALATIANS 1:15

CHAPTER 12

PAUL

Set Apart Unto God

If ever there was a person consumed with a love for Christ and the Father, it was the apostle Paul. While riding to Damascus in a religious fervor to imprison and slaughter Christians, Saul (later called Paul) had an experience that would forever change him. Saul was a very zealous person, a Pharisee who knew a lot about God, but he never knew Him intimately. It was on the road to Damascus that Saul met the Lord. That encounter was so intense that it propelled him into a passionate pursuit of the Father's heart.

As you read through the book of Acts, you become familiar with some of Paul's missionary journeys, and the churches he established. But to really see his heart and to appreciate his pursuit of God requires that we look at what he taught others. It is important to note that the apostle Paul wrote the majority of the epistles (letters) in the New Testament. Paul, who had received his teaching from personal encounters from the risen Lord, taught church doctrine, personal conduct and other weighty spiritual issues.

Scripture indicates that Paul disappeared from the church scene for a number of years. Scholars believe that it was during this time that the Lord revealed to him much of the New Testament teaching and theology we have from Paul. Paul said, "And I knew such a man, (whether in the body, or out of the body, I cannot tell: God knoweth;) How that he was caught up into paradise, and heard unspeakable words, which it is not lawful for a man to utter" (2 Cor. 12:3–4). Paul was, of course, speaking of his own experience. What he heard from God was so holy and sacred that he was not permitted to share it. I believe that Paul waded out so deeply into the river of God's presence that it went over his head and carried him to a place where he was lost in His presence. Paul sought God, not for knowledge, but for intimate friendship and communion. He had one motive, one aim— to draw closer to Him and to give his whole life to the pursuit of God.

In Paul's letter to the Philippians he wrote, "According to my earnest expectation and my hope, that in nothing I shall be ashamed, but that with all boldness, as always, so now also Christ shall be magnified in my body, whether it be by life, or by death" (Phil. 1:20). You know that you are drawing close to God when you become more God-conscious than self-conscious. Paul was at the place where he was no longer concerned about what was in it for himself; he wanted to know what was in it for God. Paul continued, "For to me to live is Christ, and to die is gain" (v. 21). This describes a life wholly given over to the Father. Paul knew that to depart from this life resulted in his gain. He writes of his conflict: "For I am in a strait betwixt two, having a desire to depart, and to be with Christ; which is far better" (v. 23). Paul was torn between two desires: one was to depart this world and be with Christ; the other was to remain on the earth and complete his calling—which he realized was more needful. I believe Paul found himself in the same place that Enoch did. Perhaps the difference in their outcome was the position in God each held. Paul was an apostle called to share the gospel with the church and to write much of the New Testament scriptures. Enoch, called a prophet by Jude, also had an unquenchable hunger for God. They both found themselves in a similar situation; they could not get enough of God.

We know that God took Enoch. I believe the same would have happened to Paul had he looked at the Father and said, "I just want to be with You." But Paul knew it was better for the church for him to stay; and he made the unselfish choice to do so. God used Paul to establish the church, but Paul's desire to depart and be with God is typical of those who get lost in His presence. I have met people who desire to be with God because they are tired of the world system or tired of dealing with life; that is not the same. Paul's desire was a result of spending time in His presence. Paul wanted to be with Christ because he was so in love with Him. When I pray, I tell the Father, "Lord, I long to be with You, but Lord I want to stay and complete my calling and destiny according to Your will." I realize that, as a minister and as a teacher, I have a work to complete; therefore, it is more needful that I remain. That does not keep me from pouring my heart out to the Father and telling Him how much I long to be with Him. When you are really hungry for Him, it will come out in your prayers and conversations with the Father.

What makes Paul's letter to the Philippians so awesome is that he wrote it from prison where he was incarcerated for preaching the gospel. Paul was probably in his late fifties or mid-sixties at this time. For him to still be in hot pursuit of God excites and encourages me. He continued to declare his passion for Christ: "That I may know him, and the power of his resurrection, and the fellowship of his sufferings, being made conformable unto his death" (Phil. 3:30). The word Paul used for *know* in this passage of scripture means "to become intimately acquainted with." Paul's desire was to progressively draw closer to the Lord. That desire was birthed years earlier, when Christ met him on the road to Damascus. It never faded, grew cold or common. I hope that you are starting to see a pattern here. We should not be on fire one minute, then cold the next. Our relationship with Christ should continue to grow and mature. If we are hot one day and cold the next, it may be the result of allowing circumstances to dictate our feelings toward God. I would do some serious soul-searching if that were the case.

Our relationship with Christ should never become mundane or boring. The Father has so much that He wants to say to us. In my eleven-plus years of marriage, I have never been bored speaking to my wife. How much more is that the case with the Father? There is no room for boredom when you are in an exciting relationship! I love my wife more now than ever before; I do not experience periods when I do not love her or feel less love or desire toward her. The same is true of my children and my parents. It definitely should not be the case with the Father that our love would lessen. If it were, then I would say that we have yet to experience a relationship with Him. A shallow relationship is one in which we give our all for a short period of time, then grow cold to a point of walking away or staying ineffective. A shallow relationship is one that resembles a roller coaster—up one moment, then down the next; never stable. This continual up-and-down relationship renders you ineffective for His kingdom.

It is possible to develop a closeness with God that continually grows and becomes more fervent. Yes, you may stumble or have battles, but you will pick yourself up and keep on going. You will never turn back. The Lord spoke to me about Philippians 3:10 one day saying, "First salvation, then intimacy, then power." Salvation is the most important step, without it we cannot enjoy fellowship with the Father. We cannot have relationship or a powerful ministry without salvation. Many Christians want power without relationship, but it is not wise to seek it in that order.

One of the saddest scenes recorded in Scripture will occur on the day of judgment. Jesus said, "Many will say to me in that day, Lord, Lord, have we not prophesied in thy name? and in thy name have cast out devils? and in thy name done many wonderful works? And then will I profess unto them,

I never knew you: depart from me, ye that work iniquity" (Matt. 7:22–23). Accomplishing things for God is not as important as knowing Him. Paul's desire was relationship first; then he walked in power. Too many people want anointing for a "large ministry," or they want to do great things for God, but they neglect the most important part— intimacy with Him. How can we share His heart if we have never felt His heartbeat? How can we share His words if we have not heard Him ourselves? We want to give people a word from the Lord and be powerful in our delivery, but neglect the very thing that will make that happen—intimate relationship with the Lord.

Paul then continued, "I follow after, if that I may apprehend that for which also I am apprehended of Christ Jesus" (Phil. 3:12). Paul was saying, "I want to take hold of and grasp Him who has taken hold of me, which is Christ Jesus!" Paul knew that Christ longed for intimate communion with him, so he wanted to chase after Christ just as Christ had pursued him. It has been said that communication is a two-way street. That is true with intimacy also. Intimacy is both received and given; otherwise it is not intimacy. God has shown His desire toward us through Christ; the ball is now in our court, so to speak. We either pursue Him or walk away. He has made His intentions known to us; so the question is, how are you going to respond? I know for myself that I am going to follow Paul's lead and reach for Christ—reach for Him who has reached out and taken hold of me!

Paul then said, "I press toward the mark for the prize of the high calling of God in Christ Jesus" (v. 14). Paul was pressing forward with one goal in mind: to attain Christ Jesus. What is our goal in pursuing Him? Is it for revelation knowledge? Is it for power, prestige or even for a greater anointing? Or is our one aim and desire to attain Christ? It should be! That is my desire! Yes, I received Christ at salvation, but I want to become intimately acquainted with Him. Praise God for revelation insight into His Word. I am thankful for a greater anointing for prayer and ministry of the

Word, but those are just benefits. My goal is to know Him. I want to draw closer still. My heartcry is, "I appreciate Your benefits, Father; but more than that, I want You!"

The apostle Paul wrote of Christ in his letter to the Colossians, "In whom are hid all the treasures of wisdom and knowledge" (Col. 2:3). The depths of God's hidden treasures are too great for us to ever explore completely. Each time we wade out into the river of His presence, it will be new to us. We will never tire of being alone with Him because what He has to share with us will be fresh every day. That is what Paul meant when he wrote to the Colossians concerning the Father and Christ. Just as close friendships remain vibrant for years, so much more should our relationship with the Father remain fresh and exciting. If it becomes complacent or dry, it is because we have allowed it to do so. The fault lies with us, never with Him. Those who continually hunger for Him will never be dissatisfied.

Only one thing satisfies a thirsty person—cool water. Only one thing satisfies a thirsty and hungry soul—the presence of God. Jesus told the woman at the well, "Whosoever drinketh of this water shall thirst again: But whosoever drinketh of the water that I shall give him shall never thirst; but the water that I shall give him shall be in him a well of water springing up into everlasting life" (John 4:14). He was speaking of satisfying that spiritual hunger that is resident within each of us. Though Christ satisfies that inner searching and hunger, the longing for more of Him continues as we desire to know Him even more. Paul expressed that desire. I can almost hear his prayers from that jail cell now: "Father, thank You for all the insight and revelation You have given, but I want You. Thank You for the gifts of the Spirit and for my calling, but more than that, it is You I want." It was no wonder Paul admonished the Colossian Christians, "Seek those things which are above, where Christ sitteth on the right hand of God" (Col. 3:1). Paul's desire was that others would discover this same relationship that he enjoyed. He said, "Be ye followers of me, even as I also am of Christ" (1 Cor. 11:1).

My desire is to raise up an army of believers who hunger only for God. The more I read about the fathers of the faith in the Word, the hungrier I get for a similar relationship. Paul's journey began when God knocked him off his horse, and it continued for the rest of his life. Paul regretted his religious life prior to his conversion, yet he did not let the past affect his pursuit of God. Paul is a perfect example to refute the thought that God would not want to have relationship with us because of our past, as we have discussed. Not only was he a murderer of Christians, but Paul also called himself the "chief of sinners." How many people have missed out on a dynamic relationship with God because they allowed their past to stop their pursuit of Him? All of us have things in our past that we are ashamed of; however, I choose not to let that keep me from Him.

As we look at Paul's life, we get a glimpse of a man who not only loved God passionately, but whose love of God also affected his relationship with others. Paul told the Galatians how he travailed in prayer for them. (See 4:19.) Cultivating intimate relationship with God will make you a better minister. It will make you a better father, a better mother and even a better employee. Most importantly, choosing to be lost in His presence will make you a better Christian. What I mean by this is, the closer we get to Him, the more we become like Him in our attitudes and character. Jesus said, "The light of the body is the eye: therefore when thine eye is single, thy whole body also is full of light; but when thine eye is evil, thy body also is full of darkness" (Luke 11:34). Having a single eye to follow Christ fully will fill our lives with light. The apostle Paul declared: "Ye are all the children of light, and the children of the day: we are not of the night, nor of darkness" (1 Thess. 5:5). Scripture teaches that God is light and in Him is no darkness at all. (See 1 John 1:5.) It follows, therefore, that as we spend time in His presence, we will be filled with ever-increasing measures of light—the character of God.

John also wrote, "And the city had no need of the sun, neither of the moon, to shine in it: for the glory of God did

lighten it, and the Lamb is the light thereof" (Rev. 21:23).
When you study the glory of God, you get the picture that
His glory is fire and light—an extremely bright light. We see
this supernatural light when Christ was transfigured before
Peter, James, and John: "And he was transfigured before
them. His face did shine like the sun, and his clothes became
as white as the light" (Matt. 17:2, author's paraphrase). So,
naturally, the closer you get to the light, the more it illuminates through you, pushing out all darkness until you begin
to resemble Him in your words, actions, and thoughts. Paul
told the Ephesians, "For ye were sometimes darkness, but
now are ye light in the Lord: walk as children of light" (Eph.
5:8). In his letter to the Corinthian church, Paul gave simple
counsel to these Christians living in the wicked city of Corinth.
It was a prosperous city known for its commerce and also its
temples filled with prostitutes. The Corinthian Christians
were winning people to the Lord, but unfortunately the
ungodly influences around them were creeping into the
church. You only need to read Paul's letters to them to get a
glimpse of this ungodliness with which he had to deal. Here
is Paul's answer to their temptation and compromise: "But
we all, with open face beholding as in a glass the glory of the
Lord, are changed into the same image from glory to glory,
even as by the Spirit of the Lord" (2 Cor. 3:18). Paul was
reiterating what Christ lived and taught. As we come into
God's presence and abide with Him, we are impacted and
transformed by that divine presence. We know that even on a
human level we are influenced by the people we hang around.
If we want to be like Christ, Paul said to look at His glory.

As you gaze upon Him, the Father of light, you will
become like Him. You will become what you are declared to
be already—children of light. I have often prayed, "Father, I
want to get so close to You that when You look at me, You
will see the reflection of Your Son, Jesus." Paul believed it
was a person's responsibility to live for God, yet he also recognized that outside of Christ it was impossible to live the
victorious life God intended for us.

When I was young in the Lord, I realized that each time I was in church and the Spirit was moving, the desire to sin was the last thing on my mind. The struggle took place when I was at my secular job or at home doing my own thing. So I determined that if I stayed in God's presence, I would not sin. But how could I do that? I discovered the answer many years later reading Ephesians. Paul gave the Ephesians a practical teaching on practicing His presence and walking with Him all the time by "Speaking to yourselves in psalms and hymns and spiritual songs, singing and making melody in your heart to the Lord" (Eph. 5:19). I call this creating a divine atmosphere—or "throne zone"—that attracts the Father's attention. Our lives are to be a sweet fragrance, and we know that God inhabits the praises of His people. (See Psalm 22:3.)

Just as our love songs of longing and desire for God draw Him closer, so sin causes Him to pull away. What is sin? We often hear sin defined as "missing the mark," but it is more than that. Sin separates us from the Father; it opens the door to the enemy, giving him a foothold to abuse us. Sin occurs when we act out the temptations in our minds. It is when we do that which is not pleasing to God or is in violation of His Word. I maintain that it is practically impossible for that to happen if we practice His presence as Paul taught. If our thoughts are on Him, then we will not think about those things with which the enemy bombards our minds. If our focus is on Him and we are walking in the Spirit, there is less chance of us missing the mark. That is not to say we will live perfect lives or never sin. I am not teaching that, nor do I believe it. I do believe, though, that there is less chance of us missing the mark as we cling to God, continually pursuing His presence.

I realize that as long as we live in this fleshly body, we will have to deal with the flesh and things that negatively affect it to the point of grieving Him; however, being in His presence daily will help us to become overcomers. We will not look for satisfaction in drugs or alcohol. Pornography will not have a grip on us as we lose ourselves in Him. We will want to live victorious lives that are pleasing to Him. Paul taught us how to do so. My desire as a pastor and evangelist is to lead people into His presence so they can be changed from glory to glory. Does God love us any less when we stumble or fall? No, of course, not! His love is everlasting! Keep in mind though, that there will be those He also loves, but from whom He must turn away in the final judgment because of His holy nature.

There is much to learn from Paul's life and his walk with God. I encourage you to take the time to read his letters and allow the Holy Spirit to stir you up in your walk with God. My sincere prayer and desire is that you will practice what Paul taught, and that you will learn to practice living in God's presence. Get alone with God. Have a time of intimate communion and fellowship with Him. Open your heart to Him, and sing love songs to Him. Voice your desire for Him—only Him. Let it flow from your heart, not just your lips. Lose yourself in His presence. As you do, you will feel His arms wrapping around you and pulling you closer to Him until the fragrance of your worship is mingled and lost in the fragrance of His presence. The Father is waiting to hear your love songs to Him. Are you ready to lose yourself in His presence? Like Paul, God wants to take you to depths that you have never experienced before. What are you waiting for? Cry out to Him and let the pursuit begin!

*"And let them make
me a sanctuary that I may dwell
among them."*

—Exodus 25:8

CHAPTER 13

The Tabernacle

As I mentioned earlier, the only way to experience an intimate friendship with the Father is to go beyond the veil. This reference to "going beyond the veil" comes as a description from the Old Testament wilderness tabernacle of Moses. The tabernacle was God's way to dwell among His chosen people, Israel, while they journeyed through the wilderness on their way to the Promised Land. The tabernacle and its contents symbolically pointed to the coming of Christ and Calvary many years later. The wonderful types and shadows found in Moses' tabernacle reveal to us the depth of relationship the Father longs to have with each of us.

The key to understanding our longing for God and the type of relationship He desires with us can be found by looking at this tabernacle. Perhaps you are familiar with the structure and content of this tabernacle; but because there is so much to learn from it regarding our relationship with God, we will consider it briefly. The wilderness tabernacle was divided into three main areas. Each area was separated from the other by fine linen, animal skins, or boards of wood. A wall of fine linen, in turn, enclosed those three areas. When it was erected, the whole structure was rectangular in shape. There was only one doorway into the tabernacle and each succeeding area.

The first area was called the outer court and contained two important components. First there was the brazen altar on which the priest offered sacrifices and offerings, depending on which holy day it was. The other important piece of furniture located in the outer court was called the brazen laver—a large bowl that contained water and was made with mirrors on the inside. The laver was placed in front of the entrance to the holy place, the second room within the enclosed area of the tabernacle.

After making the sacrifice or offering, the priest would step to the laver and look into the mirrors. He then proceeded to wash his hands and feet with the water. Afterwards, He would enter the inner court, or holy place, through a veil that served as a door. There were three items of furniture in this inner court. One was the table of shewbread, also known as the bread of His presence, containing twelve loaves of bread. Then there was the golden candlestick, composed of seven oil-filled "candles"; one tall candlestick in the center with three branches coming from either side. Directly ahead, placed in front of another veil, was an altar, known as the altar of incense.

Beyond the altar of incense was the veil that covered the innermost court of the tabernacle, known as the holy of holies. It was there that the ark of the covenant was placed, where God Himself dwelt. This veil, which separated people from the presence of God, was four to six inches thick. It covered the only entrance into the holy of holies. In order to get into this innermost court, the high priest—the only one allowed into the holy of holies—had to go through the first two areas of the tabernacle, completing all the necessary requirements of the law. You will remember that the ark was the symbol of God's abiding presence. What an awesome and, as we will see, a fearful thing it must have been to go beyond the veil. This was the place where God Himself would meet with the high priest—only one day a year, on the Day of Atonement. Only Moses, God's friend, was permitted to go beyond the veil whenever he chose. This was the place Moses loved; this was the secret place of Jehovah, the place where only a few were allowed to go.

We have discussed some who went beyond the ordinary into an extraordinary relationship with the Father. Although some of them were pursuing the Father many years before the tabernacle was built, they got so close to Him that, in a real sense, they went "beyond the veil." They went beyond the level of relationship with God that most others attain, enjoying extraordinary communion with God.

God's desire is and always has been to tabernacle or dwell with His creation. He has longed to commune and fellowship with us, face to face. That special relationship with God suffered a devastating blow when man fell into sin. It was never God's intention to remain hidden and out of reach from our grasp behind a veil. Since God cannot dwell together with sinful man, the only way under the Old Testament law to get back into a right relationship with the Father was through a series of rituals and sacrifices. These rituals and sacrifices were removed by the work of atonement through Jesus Christ.

In our brief look at the tabernacle, we will catch a glimpse of what lies ahead for those believers who are hungry for relationship with God. God's original plan, as seen in the Garden of Eden, was to walk with His creation without barriers or walls. Because of sin, it became necessary to separate Himself from people. The tabernacle was God's way to once again be able to dwell among His people, yet even this did not allow for the closeness He desired. The problem was the sin that separated the people from God. Only by following the strict requirements of the law could atonement be made for their sin, as the high priest entered beyond the veil one day a year, on the Day of Atonement.

Only through Christ's atonement at Calvary, because of the sacrificial death of Christ, could that veil be finally torn in two so that you and I have free access into the very presence of God. The blood of Christ has atoned once and for all for sin. Those who receive Christ as Savior have free access into the very presence of God. Yet, sadly, few move into the place of intimate communion with the Father that Christ's death provided for us. I want more of Him; I want to go beyond the veil and into His awesome, incredible presence!

In Moses' tabernacle, every day a priest would enter the holy place and put fresh bread on the table of shewbread. Then the candlestick would be lit and incense would be placed on the altar of incense. A sweet fragrance would fill the room as the incense was burned. This was done every day throughout the year. Then, on the Day of Atonement, the high priest would be permitted to go beyond the veil into the holy of holies. This responsibility was one the high priest highly anticipated, yet greatly feared. Death would result if the sacrifices were not properly completed.

Through the centuries, the ark of the covenant remained the place of God's presence. However, there were times when the enemies of God's people captured the ark, resulting in years without a place of God's presence. During King David's reign, when the ark of covenant was recovered, the ark was placed in a tent and again became the central place of worship for Israel. It is interesting that there was no veil in David's tent separating the people from the presence of God. David commanded that continual worship and praise be offered before the presence of the Lord day and night. (See 1 Chronicles 16:40.)

Later, when David desired to build a house for the Lord, God responded that he could gather the materials and that his son would build the temple. David's son, Solomon, built a magnificent temple and placed the ark of the covenant there. One day I asked the Lord why He wanted to go back to being behind a veil, and the Lord said, "People sometimes mishandle that with which they become familiar, and if you mishandle what is holy, you are in danger of judgment." We saw that reality played out in the lives of the two sons of Aaron, Nadab and Abihu, who died when they offered strange fire before the Lord, and in the life of Uzzah, who died when he touched the ark.

Scripture tells us that when Christ was crucified, the veil in the temple was torn from the top to the bottom. (See Matthew 27:51.) God was letting all of mankind know that Christ had just opened a way for all persons to come beyond the veil into His presence and enjoy sweet communion with Him. What was only available to a few in the Old Testament was now available to everyone who would accept Christ as Savior.

Why go beyond the veil? The primary reason is that the Father, the Creator of the universe, longs for fellowship and communion with His children. Within every relationship, there must be growth in order for it to flourish and mature. So it is with our relationship with God. We either choose to move beyond the outer court into the holy of holies, or we choose not to. That is why He says, "He that cometh to God must believe that he is, and that he is a rewarder of them that diligently seek Him" (Heb. 11:6). To diligently seek something means to crave it, to require it, to search out and investigate it. Desperately hungry people search God out; they crave Him. Do you crave relationship with God? Do you long for Him desperately?

Sometimes I compare the three areas of the tabernacle to the phases we go through in life and in our relationships. It actually offers the perfect illustration in the progression of our relationship with the Father, as we will discuss in the following chapters. You can see the natural progression in a couple as they start as friends, then move on to romance, then intimacy within marriage. If a relationship jumps right into intimacy without first the friendship and the romance, it will likely come to an end because there is no solid foundation for the relationship. Our relationship with God is also progressive. Jesus illustrated this natural progression for growth when He said, "For the earth bringeth forth fruit of herself; first the blade, then the ear, after that the full corn in the ear" (Mark 4:28).

Understanding the principle of growth in God, we can learn more from the symbolism of the tabernacle of how to come into intimate relationship with God. It is God who is calling His bride to go beyond the veil into His secret place, to the place where He alone dwells and waits for us. This is a place revealed only to those who seek Him diligently. Are you hungry for Him? If you are willing to pay the price for closeness with the Father, which only a few have experienced, then do not hesitate! The Father is waiting for you!

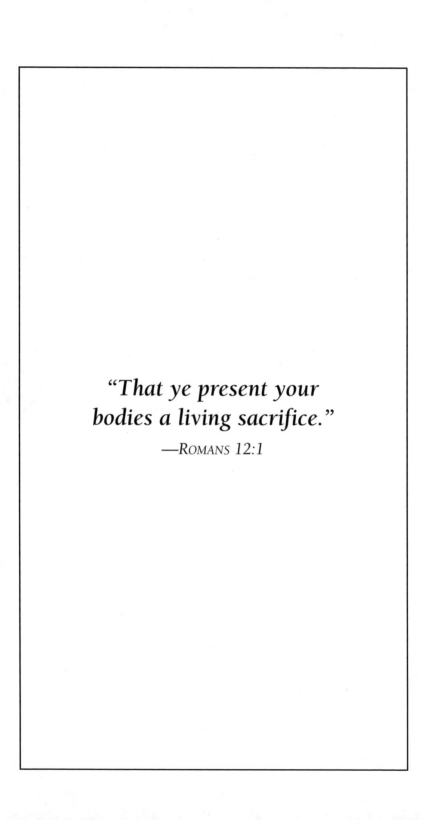

*"That ye present your
bodies a living sacrifice."*
—ROMANS 12:1

CHAPTER 14

THE OUTER COURT

Our First Step

As we discussed in the last chapter, there were three sections to the wilderness tabernacle—the outer court, the inner court and the holy of holies. You could not get to the holy of holies, the place of His presence, without first going through the other two sections. As we mentioned, the symbolism of the tabernacle points toward Christ and the sacrifice of Calvary. As there was only one entrance into the outer court of the tabernacle, so there is only one way to the Father, which is through Jesus Christ. The priest would enter what was called the outer court of the tabernacle to offer sacrifices on the altar of burnt offering. The law prescribed different requirements for each sacrifice and offering.

We take our first step toward the Father when we accept Christ as our Savior. That acceptance of Him and the work He accomplished on the cross is the first and most important step. Just as there can be no honeymoon without first a marriage, so we cannot move into intimacy with the Father until we are joined to Him through Christ. We are married to

Christ through our acceptance of His sacrificial death for our sins. We see an example of this union that the Father longs for in the book of Hosea. The Lord says, "And I will betroth thee unto me for ever; yea, I will betroth thee unto me in righteousness, and in judgment, and in lovingkindness, and in mercies. I will even betroth thee unto me in faithfulness: and thou shalt know the Lord" (Hos. 2:19–20). We cannot know Him until we are married or joined to Him!

In the New Testament, the apostle Paul wrote concerning this marriage relationship: "Wherefore, my brethren, ye also are become dead to the law by the body of Christ; that ye should be married to another, even to him who is raised from the dead, that we should bring forth fruit unto God" (Rom. 7:4). The fruit of a married couple is children; the result of an intimate and close relationship. The fruit we bear for the Father is also the result of an intimate and close relationship with Him. He does not want us to draw close just for intimate fellowship, but also to bear fruit unto Him. Even Jesus taught us the importance of bearing fruit: "Herein is my Father glorified, that ye bear much fruit, so shall you be my disciples" (John 15:8). He was, of course, speaking of the things we would accomplish for Him. It is important to understand that we cannot know Him beyond head knowledge unless we draw closer to Him. The tabernacle illustrates this principle for us. Just as it was necessary for the priest to go through a process of progressively getting closer to the presence of God as he made his way through the tabernacle, so it is with us.

When the priest entered the outer court, he had to offer a sacrifice at the altar of burnt offering. The altar of burnt offering symbolizes for believers our need to die to our self-life; our motives and selfish desires are to be placed on that altar. Unless everything was done according to God's requirement, the priest would not be allowed to move on. So it is with us today; unless we decrease and allow His life to increase in us, we will never be able to draw as close to Him as He longs for us to be. Our churches are filled with people who "hang out" around this altar. Some stand close; others stand back, but they will not place their self-life on the altar. They want to move on with God. They want a greater commitment *from* Him in their daily affairs, but they are not willing to get on the altar and make a commitment *to* Him.

There were some sacrifices that required an animal to be skinned and certain parts removed. This speaks to us of laying aside those things that easily distract us and hinder our walk with God. To become a living sacrifice (see Romans 12:1), is something we must do daily. I said in an earlier chapter that the closer we get to God, the more sensitive we become to those things that grieve Him. Part of being a living sacrifice is laying on the altar those things in our lives that grieve Him. If our lives are to be a sweet fragrance unto Him, we must allow the fire of God to remove the things that foul up our lives! The question we must answer is what we are willing to lay down on the altar for Him. Are we willing to remove the things that pollute our lives? Living the crucified life is not always enjoyable, but the rewards are incredible! The Father expects us to lay aside those things that grieve Him and that keep us from moving into more intimate relationship with Him. Are we willing to do it? Or will we become like so many others—satisfied that we are in the outer court, watching those who are "privileged" go into the inner court?

Christians who are satisfied with hanging out in the outer court are usually those who are shallow and easily distracted. They are the ones Paul referred to as being babies and carnal, still in need of milk and unable to handle the deeper things of God. (See 1 Corinthians 3.) The deeper things of God cannot be found in the outer court. The outer court is the place of beginnings! As such, we should be willing to grow in Christ and move on. Christians in the outer court are more caught up in personalities, chasing one shooting-star ministry after another. Their continual dwelling in the outer court proves that they are not caught up with Christ! Oh, they will tell you how much they want Him when they are in church or around other Christians. They will say how much they desire Him, but each time you meet them, they are still in the same condition and place as they were before. Though their lips say one thing, what is in their heart is evident. They do not really want to draw closer.

It will cost you something to know God as did Moses, Abraham, John, and Paul. You cannot just get in a prayer line and have some hotshot preacher lay hands on you and get it! I do not recall Paul ever saying in any of his letters, "When I come to town, anybody who would like to get what I've got can just come see me and I'll lay hands on them and transfer it to them." No, it does not work that way. Yet you will see that in the outer court Christian; they are always looking for a way to get from God what only comes from dying to self.

An outer court Christian usually has no root in any particular church; therefore, they jump from one church to another, never settling or committing to a church or a pastor. The reason we lose so many new converts is because they never get beyond the altar. They come close; they have accepted Christ. Unfortunately many go back into the world, either because of not being taught or because they just do not want to pay the price of servanthood. If a person is hungry for God and His presence, they will willingly get on the altar and say, "Lord, it might hurt, but remove from my life those things of sin and separation." It is when you get to that place of yielding yourself to Him and placing your life on the altar, wanting Him more than your comfort, that you are ready to move on with God.

After sacrificing the burnt offering, the priest would then walk to the brazen laver, made of mirrors and filled with water. The priest would wash his hands and sprinkle water on his feet. This washing symbolizes the continual washing of our lives by the Word of God, as Paul declared: "That he might sanctify and cleanse it [the church of Christ] with the washing of water by the word" (Eph. 5:26). The priest washed his hands and his feet. This represents the need for our works and walk to be covered by the Word of God. The priest was going into the presence of God carrying the blood of the sacrifice. If we are to carry the Holy things of God, it must be done with clean hands. The psalmist David wrote, "Who shall ascend into the hill of the Lord? or who shall stand in his holy place? He that hath clean hands, and a pure heart" (Ps. 24:3–4).

Does God love us unconditionally? Yes, of course; but some things are only attained as we allow the Spirit of God to reveal hidden sin in us and as we choose to allow Him to remove it. God does clean us up, but the Word makes it clear that it is our responsibility to make the choice to renounce sin and turn from it. The priest would look into the brazen laver made of mirrors, and he could see any flaws and dirt that needed to be cleaned up. God always brings us to the brazen laver and shows us those things in our hearts that need to be dealt with. As believers, going to the laver is like looking at ourselves in the mirror and seeing what the Holy Spirit sees. This is a lifelong requirement! It requires living a life of repentance, progressively drawing closer to Him and becoming more like Him in our walk.

Sometimes seeing what the Holy Spirit sees can be a painful experience—as He shows us things that maybe we had no idea offended or grieved Him. But the purpose is always to make us more like Him. God loves us too much to allow us to harbor things in our lives that He wants removed, so He leads us to the brazen laver and causes us to see what breaks His heart. Then He gives us the strength to remove it, what-ever it may be. Whether it is a bad attitude or some secret sin, each trip to the laver is an opportunity to see those hidden areas. Not everything revealed is sin; there may be past hurts that need to be dealt with because they are stopping us from drawing closer to Him. Regardless of what the Holy Spirit reveals to you at the laver, learn to yield to Him so you can draw closer. Unfortunately, many Christians in the outer court are content to hold on to their secret sins and inner strife. Yet, the Father continues to beckon us to come beyond the veil into His presence. All the changes that take place in our lives are so the Father can get the maximum glory from our lives and to allow us to enjoy His presence.

The outer court is our first step in pursuing intimate friendship with the Father, but it is not the only step. The greatest danger you will face is the temptation to remain in the place where you are currently, without growing. Do not be satisfied with mediocrity! Push on beyond the brazen altar to the brazen laver. Allow the Holy Spirit to reveal those things that the Father wants to remove, then do not resist, but yield in obedience to Him. The purpose is to come forth as gold tried in the fire. Do you hear Him calling you?

After washing his hands and feet and looking at his reflection to make certain everything was in order, the priest was ready to continue his journey into the inner court. Before entering, he would do two things. First, he would do a quick mental check to make certain that all instructions as required by God had been followed. The priest would then tie a rope around his ankle. Placed on the fringes of his priestly garments were little bells. As he performed his services in the inner court and eventually in the holy of holies, those bells would tinkle. If they stopped, it was a sign that the priest had died because of failing to be obedient in all the holy requirements. If the priest died, those in the outer court would pull his body out.

If you think as a Christian that we can just prance into the holy things of God without thought or care, you have misunderstood His holiness. Paul wrote, "Follow peace with all men, and holiness, without which no man shall see the Lord" (Heb. 12:14); and again, "For God hath not called us unto uncleanness, but unto holiness" (1 Thess. 4:7). Holiness means purity of heart and life. Jesus said, "Blessed are the pure in heart: for they shall see God" (Matt. 5:8). The word translated *pure* means "purified by fire"! The closer we get to the fire of His presence, the more He burns out of us in order for us to continue to draw closer to Him. The Father is waiting for you to come closer.

Using the analogy of a wedding, we would be married to Him in the outer court. Moving forward after the ceremony, we would enter the banquet hall, or inner court. Of course we are en route to the holy of holies, the honeymoon suite.

*"Let us draw near
with a true heart."*

—HEBREWS 10:22

CHAPTER 15

THE INNER COURT

Going Yet Deeper

As the priest passed through the doorway into the inner court, his way was guided only by the light from the golden candlestick that had been lit earlier that morning. The aroma of fresh bread filled the room. He then walked ahead to the altar of incense and took a burning coal and placed it in a golden censer he was holding. The censer was a golden, circular-like tube. He then sprinkled some specially made holy incense on the hot coals in his censer and a beautiful fragrance filled the room.

When you move from the outer court into the inner court, also known as the holy place, it is just another step into the deeper things of God. Like the river in Ezekiel, you have moved from ankle-deep water into knee-deep water, yet there is much more to experience in the depths of God's presence.

Remember, in the outer court Christ is predominately known as the sacrificial Lamb. The outer-court Christian is aware that they have been forgiven of their sins and are joined to Christ (married to Him). We also saw that the outer court can be a painful place because it is there that we begin the process of dying to self. Having sins and idols exposed at the laver can be painful, but enduring the cleansing process there allows you to progress further.

You now stand in the inner court. The table of shewbread is a type of Christ in that He is the Bread of Life. Jesus said, "For the bread of God is he which cometh down from heaven, and giveth life unto the world. Then said they unto him, Lord, evermore give us this bread. And Jesus said unto them, I am the bread of life: he that cometh to me shall never hunger; and he that believeth on me shall never thirst" (John 6:33–35). It is here in the inner court that a person begins a closer walk with the Lord, partaking of the fresh bread. That freshness in your relationship with God should be new every day. The bread in the inner court was changed out every day. The main reason for revival is to refocus our attention on Christ and get us back to a place of freshness with Him. The fact that it was the responsibility of the priest to keep the bread fresh every day speaks to us today that we must not let our relationship with the Father grow stale or common; it must be renewed daily. Some may ask if that is possible. The answer, of course, is "Yes it is."

Consider the Pharisees in Jesus' day. Their relationship was dead and lifeless. It was based on form and dead works, covered in decaying rituals. Their deadness to God was the result of becoming too familiar with the holy and taking it for granted.

The day Christ was transfigured before Peter, James, and John, they all saw His glory manifested; yet a few nights later Peter denied even knowing Him! As humans, we are subject to being flaky at times. That is why we must safeguard ourselves against such failures. A good cure for becoming like the Pharisees of Jesus' day is to ask God for a deep hunger for Him. A consuming hunger for Him will keep Christ fresh in our lives because we will never be satisfied with what we have. A hungry person wants more fresh bread. When they get it, they want more. Jesus said, "Blessed are they which do hunger and thirst after righteousness: for they shall be filled" (Matt. 5:6). Jesus knew that only one thing would satisfy the hunger pains in a person, and that was Him, the fresh Bread of Life. If you are chewing on stale, lifeless bread or moldy bread delivered by others, then you need to get to the inner court, the place of fresh bread.

The other item we have mentioned that was in the inner court or holy place of the tabernacle was the golden candlestick. It had one main centerpiece and three branches on each side for a total of seven lights. On the top of each candlestick was a small bowl that contained specially made oil, which was considered most holy. So holy in fact that God forbid the making of it for any other purpose other than what it was used for in the inner court. This oil is a type of the Holy Spirit. Those who try to mimic the Holy Spirit or push Him aside, rather than follow His leading, are using the oil for their own purposes. God will not tolerate such disrespect for His holiness; it's either done God's way or no way!

The candlestick was lit every morning and evening, providing the only light in the inner court. This light speaks to us of the illumination of the Holy Spirit in our lives. The candlestick, representing the life of the Holy Spirit, illuminates the bread, representing Jesus, on the table of shewbread. This is how we receive insight and revelation from the Word of God. The Word by itself is very important, but unless the Holy Spirit illumines it and gives us understanding, we will never comprehend the message of the Word or the Author. Jesus promised us the help of the Holy Spirit: "But the Comforter, which is the Holy Ghost, whom the Father will send in my name, he shall teach you all things, and bring all things to your remembrance, whatsoever I have said unto you" (John 14:26). Again, we are told the Holy Spirit will teach us: "But the anointing which ye have received of him abideth in you, and ye need not that any man teach you: but as the same anointing teacheth you of all things, and is truth, and is no lie, and even as it hath taught you, ye shall abide in him" (1 John 2:27).

I realize that the candlestick could also represent Christ, who is the Light of the world. I believe, however, it more correctly represents the work of the Holy Spirit as we have discussed it. Since Christ is the express image of the Godhead, and God is three in one, this overlapping of symbolism, in a way, gives us understanding of the trinity. It is the Holy Spirit who convicts us of sin and brings us to the Father. It is the Holy Spirit who prompts us to draw closer to the Father and also sheds light on the Word. And Christ is the Word. Understanding this is of utmost importance in helping us to develop a relationship and sensitivity to the Holy Spirit.

When a person steps from the outer court into the inner court, their relationship with the Father takes on a deeper meaning. I liken it to going to the marriage banquet hall after the wedding ceremony. It is the place where you are enjoying fellowship and being with each other, yet it is not as intimate as the honeymoon suite. What happens in the inner court is to prepare us to pursue relationship with the Father more deeply. It is in the inner court, as you partake of the Bread of Life, Jesus, that you want more or *should* want more. However, it is easy to get so caught up in what is going on in the inner court that you become satisfied with your experience there. Most Christians are in the outer court; some draw closer to the point of entering into the inner court. Of those who enter the holy place, fewer still move beyond the veil into the holy of holies.

The other item of importance in the inner court is the altar of incense, which represents our prayers and worship. Our lives are to be a sweet fragrance of praise unto the Father. He longs for our worship—our songs of love and desire—to be offered up to Him. In Psalms it is written, "O come, let us worship and bow down: let us kneel before the LORD our maker" (Ps. 95:6). As I said earlier, worship births intimacy, and intimacy births worship. Worship is love songs sung to the Father. The Holy Spirit told me one day, "Worship, when pure and true, is a result of true affection, gratefulness and recognition of One greater and higher than you and for no other reason than that He is." It is not something mandated by God, but is a natural out-flowing of our love and relationship with the One who gave His all to us, expecting nothing in return.

The altar of incense had pure holy incense sprinkled on it every morning. The aroma of that incense filled the room and lingered on the priest. You can always tell when someone has been alone with the Father; there is an aroma of His presence that lingers with them. How sad that many Christians flock to hear all the popular speakers, waiting in line for hours just to get close and hear what they have to say. Why? It is because they want to smell the aroma of where these ministers have been. They are so hungry, yet they are not willing to go there themselves. There is a price to pay to go into the inner court, as evidenced by the altar of burnt offering. Many Christians would rather hang out in the outer court and wait for someone who has been in the inner court to walk by so they can smell that aroma.

When the high priest entered the inner court on the Day of Atonement on his way to the holy of holies, he would go to the altar of incense with a golden censer and take some of the coals from the altar of incense and place them in his censer. Then he would take some of the holy incense, specially made and beaten into a fine powder, and he would sprinkle it on the hot coals in his censer. He did this according to the instructions laid out by God, "And he shall put the incense upon the fire before the LORD, that the cloud of the incense may cover the mercy seat that is upon the testimony, that he die not" (Lev. 16:13).

After he sprinkled the incense on the coals in his censer, the priest would drop to his knees in fear and reverence before the veil separating him from the holy of holies. Because there was no break in the veil, the only way to enter was on his knees. The priest would lift the veil and place the censer under it and wave it back and forth. He had to make certain, according to Levitical law, that the fragrant smoke filled the holy of holies before he entered; otherwise he would die. His flesh could not be seen, and only worship could lift him into the presence of the Father.

Today our right to come before the Father's throne is made possible only by the blood of Jesus. The means to the throne is worship. Before a person can move beyond the veil, they must grasp all that is available in the inner court. They must recognize Christ as the Bread of Life. The Holy Spirit spoke to me not long ago and said, "Looking at the bread won't do you any good; you have to partake of it. It's when you break the bread, when you partake of it, that you come into an intimate knowing of Jesus." Shortly after Christ was risen from the dead, two of His followers were walking on the road to Emmaus. (See Luke 24.) They did not recognize Him until they stopped for lunch and He took some bread, broke it and blessed it. We read, "And they told what things were done in the way, and how He was known of them in breaking of bread" (Luke 24:35). If we are to draw closer to Him, we must partake of Him! Also, in the inner court, we must seek and obey the illumination of the Holy Spirit, and we must learn to make worship and communion a lifestyle.

Christians who reject the deeper things of God, such as the baptism of the Spirit, should not be shunned or looked down upon by those of us who do believe and have experienced the Holy Spirit's baptism. I believe that going from the outer court to the inner court is still possible for those who do not believe in the baptism of the Spirit; but unless they accept everything in the inner court, they cannot move on into the deeper things of God. We cannot experience the fullness of His presence if we reject the work of the Holy Spirit, the very One who reveals His awesome presence to us.

The priest could not go beyond the veil into the holy of holies until he had finished all that was required in the inner court. Jesus said, "He that believeth on me, as the scripture hath said, out of his belly shall flow rivers of living water. (But this spake he of the Spirit, which they that believe on him should receive: for the Holy Ghost was not yet given; because that Jesus was not yet glorified)" (John 7:38). For someone to say they have the baptism of the Holy Spirit, and yet their lives do not overflow in wonderful exuberant praise and worship, shows they do not have what Christ promised and what is found only in the inner court. Therefore, they will be limited in their walk with the Father. Jesus thought it important enough that He told the disciples not to enter into ministry without first waiting for the promised outpouring. He said for them to remain in Jerusalem and "wait for the promise of the Father, which, saith he, ye have heard of me. For John truly baptized with water; but ye shall be baptized with the Holy Ghost not many days hence" (Acts 1:4–5). Prior to this He had breathed on them and said "Receive the Holy Spirit," which is the coming of salvation. Yet, afterwards He told them there was a baptism with the Holy Ghost awaiting them. This baptism, which they had not yet experienced, is what is found in the inner court. We either move on into the deeper things of the Spirit, or we do not; however, the consequence of not allowing the Spirit to envelope us is to not move any closer to the Father. Many Christians are happy with that, but they are missing much more that God has to offer. If we are to move beyond the veil, we must learn to hold to Christ, the bread, to allow the light of the Holy Spirit, the candlestick, and learn to lose ourselves in communion and worship at the altar of incense.

Now the high priest would be on his knees, with one hand under the veil, waving the censer back and forth. By this time the priest no doubt was shaking with fear. He would be feeling not only a reverential fear but also a terrible, awful fear that grips the entire being. It is that kind of fear that the writer of Hebrews said believers do not have to worry about: "Let us therefore come *boldly* unto the throne of grace that we may obtain mercy, and find grace to help in time of need" (Heb. 4:16). The definition of the word *boldly* in this verse means "without fear"; not without reverential fear, but the fear of the unknown. We do not need to fear being rejected and struck down as sons and daughters of the new covenant in Christ.

However, as the high priest was on his knees, his whole body shook with fear. If even one instruction had been followed incorrectly, he would die. No doubt, when he had kissed his wife and children that morning, it was without the assurance that he would see them again. As he knelt there he went over in his mind again each important step of the process beginning in the outer court. Despite his great fear of the unknown and the fear of having to face a holy God, he crawled into the holy of holies. He was at the point of no return, about to get lost, if only for a moment, in the very presence of God. In an earlier chapter I mentioned the river of God's presence. The altar of burnt offering can be likened to being ankle deep; the laver could be likened to being knee deep; the inner court could be likened to being waist deep; and now, the priest was about to go in over his head. These were waters to swim in. (See Ezekiel 47.)

Do you feel God tugging at your heart? There is an inward tugging drawing you yet closer to an encounter with the Father. You are about to enter into a place where few others have walked. It is the place where Enoch and Paul walked and did not want to leave. As with Moses, the Lord is saying, "There is a place beside Me where you can stand." Are you hungry? Do you want to go beyond the veil? There is only one physical position appropriate for beyond the veil— that is on our faces in awe. The precious blood of Jesus has paved the way, so you and I could make the journey. The way to approach is through intimate worship. Do not hesitate. Begin to fill the room with the fragrant incense of your worship. He is waiting for you.

"And the Lord spake unto Moses face to face as a man speaketh unto his friend."

—EXODUS 33:11

CHAPTER 16

FACE TO FACE

Going Beyond the Veil

As the priest entered the holy of holies, he stood before the ark of the covenant and sprinkled it seven times with the blood he brought with him. During this time the cloud of God's presence was over the tabernacle. Then suddenly the fire of almighty God would fall on the holy of holies and His concentrated manifest presence was there on the ark, between the cherubims. The priest would be upon his face in holy reverence for the God of Israel who had manifested Himself in that place! I can only imagine what it must have been like for the priest to be there. Surely his heart would have skipped a few beats! The priest experienced what few others before him had experienced.

We are told in the Word that God is a consuming fire, yet here the priest was right next to a limited view of that fire. I say limited because the earth is not large enough to contain Him. What little glimpse anyone has ever had has almost killed him or her. Should God ever show up in all His fullness, we would most definitely drop dead on the spot!

This is the place the Father longs to bring us. This is the secret place, the place of intimate communion. The psalmist wrote, "He that dwelleth [or remains] in the secret place [the inner chamber] of the most High shall [or will] abide [spend the night] under the shadow of the Almighty!" (Ps. 91:1). God calls us to come closer into His secret place, His inner chamber, to spend the night. This is the place that we are told Moses would come to and stay. When Moses would walk out from God's presence, he had to cover his face with a veil because he glowed with the presence of God. When he came into the tabernacle, he would remove the veil and bask in the glow of God's presence.

We do not know how long the priest stayed in God's presence, but we know when he came out his clothes and hair smelled of the fragrant incense. When God draws a person beyond the veil into His presence, that person is engulfed in God's holy presence just as the priest before the ark. When that person comes out from His presence, the fragrance of that encounter lingers on him, as it did with the priest. That person will also bear the effects of being in God's presence as Moses did. Just as Moses' face shone, your life will radiate with the presence of God and it will be visible to others.

What is the fragrance? It is our lifestyle, our actions, our expressions of love. Yes, I believe that there will be the faint smell of the Father on us! When you draw so close that He hugs you, people will sense it. God longs passionately for you to draw close. Do you realize He sent Christ because He wanted to restore the relationship man had with Him in the Garden of Eden? He wants to manifest Himself to you and me. The psalmist understood this when he said: "Blessed is the man whom You choose, and causes to approach unto You. That he may dwell in Your courts, we shall be satisfied with the goodness of your house, even of Your holy temple" (Ps. 65:4, author's paraphrase). David understood this presence when he said, "Thou wilt shew me the path of life: in thy presence is fullness of joy; at thy right hand there are pleasures for evermore" (Ps. 16:11). Do you hear Him calling you?

When the high priest came out of God's presence, those in the outer court could smell the fragrance of the holy incense. They would all gather around him, hoping to catch the smell. Some would touch him, hoping that it might rub off on them. The sad thing is that we see the same thing happening in the church today. Those in the outer court clamor around those who have been beyond the veil. They could enter into His presence themselves if they were willing to start at the altar of burnt offering and passionately pursue Him. The writer of Psalms puts it so eloquently for us. Listen to his desperate cry: "How amiable are thy tabernacles, O LORD of hosts! My soul longeth, yea, even fainteth for the courts of the LORD: my heart and my flesh crieth out for the living God. Yea, the sparrow hath found an house, and the swallow a nest for herself, where she may lay her young, even thine altars, O LORD of hosts, my King, and my God. Blessed are they that dwell in thy house: they will be still praising thee. Selah" (Ps. 84:1–4).

God wants you to experience His presence. He wants to draw you closer to Him. He wants you to go beyond the veil. It is the honeymoon suite, the place of intimacy. Too many Christians are happy in the outer courts. Too many are content staying in the inner court with everything it has to offer. I can understand being satisfied in the inner court; there is much to experience at that level. But there is no excuse for staying in the outer court! Yet regardless of those places, He is waiting beyond the veil.

We miss so much when we become satisfied and content in the place where we are. We must move on to the deeper things of God. He would not have made it possible or made it so clear that He longs for us to draw closer to Him if He had wanted us to stay in one place all our lives. When two people date, they will never move on to marriage if they do not allow themselves to grow closer and experience a deeper relationship. Are you hungry for God? Do you long to experience His presence as have those before you? I am hungry for Him, and I want to see His people move beyond the mediocre into the extraordinary.

I can only imagine what would happen if God's people began pressing forward into His presence, beyond the veil. What would happen if we came forth with the fragrance of Him lingering on us? How many people's lives would be changed when they see us radiate from being alone with Him? The headlines blared, "These men have turned the world upside down!" This was spoken about the first-century church. They were able to make such an impact—able to turn the world upside down—because God so affected them in the secret place. When you study church history, you will find that those who were mightily used of Him were those who had passionately pursued Him. I honestly believe the reason our shadows do not heal anyone is because we have not been abiding in *His* shadow. What has become the exception to modern-day Christians was the norm of our spiritual forefathers. So-called scholars stand up and say, "God just doesn't do that anymore." They have no scriptural basis for their narrow-mindedness.

We have become satisfied with hanging out in the outer court and chastening those who would desire to go beyond the veil. While we debate whether a person can obtain the kind of relationship with the Father that Abraham enjoyed, God waits. Some may argue that we should not chase after signs. I agree; but it is not a sign that I want. I seek His presence. Notice that Paul was never surprised when an angel showed up to give him direction because it was the norm for him. Peter did not write a book when he saw an angel. Paul was not surprised when Christ met Him and gave him revelation insight. He was not surprised at the clarity with which he heard the Spirit. The reason is that life beyond the veil, in God's presence, should be the norm, not the exception. It should not be something that you think is only available to the "golden ones" of the church. These are the spiritual celebrities parading around the platform as if they are someone special because they know how to spin a nice phrase. The question is, do *you* know God intimately? It does not matter how much Greek and Hebrew you know if you have not been beyond the veil. Do not tell me things about God in the hope that it impresses me. I want to know Him, not just *about* Him. If there is one thing I want the church of Jesus Christ to experience, it is falling so in love with Him that they are not satisfied with where they are, but have the hunger for more of Him.

Perhaps I should clarify something. Those who are in the outer court are not any less Christian or any less loved by the Father. Yes, they may be more carnally minded or caught up in things that the world has to offer. It does not matter because Christ loves them just as much as He loves those who press on into the deeper things of God. The difference lies in their closeness to His heart. What they hear and receive from the Father will not be the same as those who press into the depths of His presence.

Are you ready to move beyond the ordinary into the extraordinary? You can have the same depth of intimate communion with the Father that those we have studied have had. The only difference between them and us is the level and intensity of their hunger. They sought God as if their very lives depended upon it! He is waiting and longing for you. You have been at the wedding in the outer court. You went to the banquet in the inner court. Now move beyond the veil into the secret place, the honeymoon suite. He is waiting to draw you closer to Him. The only place you will find him—the place few have been—is open to all who will hunger for Him. He is waiting beyond the veil where you can get so close to Him, face to face, that you will feel His breath on your cheek. Begin now to lift your voice and heart in intimate worship, filling the secret place with the incense of your worshipful desire and longing. Even now the cloud of His presence is hovering over you. The fire of His manifest presence is about to fall on your life, and you will be consumed—lost—in His presence!

*"Let Him kiss me
with the kisses of His mouth."*

—SONG OF SOLOMON 1:2

CHAPTER 17

How Hungry Are You?

When God created Adam in His image and likeness, it was not because God needed someone to serve Him or to bow before Him. Rather, the Father longed for intimate friendship and communion. When my little daughter jumps in my lap and kisses me, my heart melts. When I pray over my son and kiss him on the cheek or forehead, my heart melts. If I feel this way toward my children and I am flesh and blood, how much more does God feel for us?

I believe that when Moses spoke face to face with the Father, he could feel the breath of God. It was real when John whispered in Jesus' ear, and Jesus leaned over and whispered back in John's ear. I believe when Mary sat at His feet, she was touching them. I believe when Abraham walked with Jesus toward the city of Sodom, they walked arm in arm. I believe the reason David danced with all his might before the ark of the covenant is because he had so often danced with God in the fields as a shepherd boy. Don't you long for that?

One of the meanings of the word *worship* is "to kiss." I

realize there are those who may disagree with me, but I challenge you to go to the Word. Throughout its pages I find a God who longs for more than lip service. He wants my heart, and I intend to give it to Him. He has chased me, and I intend to chase Him. In doing so, I want to birth hunger for intimacy with God in the lives of as many people as I can.

The Song of Solomon is rich with intimate pursuit. It is a type and shadow of the kind of passionate pursuit that God longs to instill in His church. Our prayer should be, "Draw me, we will run after thee: the king hath brought me into his chambers: we will be glad and rejoice in thee, we will remember thy love more than wine: the upright love thee" (Song of Sol. 1:4). The Father wants to take us from the front room to the bedroom. Intimacy is not something you share with just anyone or everyone, nor is it appropriate activity out in the open. I will hold my wife's hand in public; I will even hug her and give her a kiss, but that is the limit of our affection in public. The best, the most precious, of our intimacy is saved for the secret place.

I will worship the Father in public and tell Him I love Him. But Jesus Himself instructed us, when we pray, to enter our closet and close the door. Some things require being alone, and God desires that we enter His secret chamber to commune with Him alone. Listen to this powerful language, "I sat down under his shadow with great delight, and his fruit was sweet to my taste" (Song of Sol. 2:3). The Father only has good things to share with you. The psalmist declared: "O taste and see that the LORD is good" (Ps. 34:8). And the apostle James wrote, "Every good gift and every perfect gift is from above, and cometh down from the Father of lights, with whom is no variableness, neither shadow of turning" (James 1:17).

The writer continues in the Song of Solomon, "He brought me to the banqueting house, and his banner over me was love" (2:4). The Father will bring you to His secret place of communion. There you will dine with Him. Do you realize how much the Father loves you? He gave us a glimpse of His great love when He sent His Son, Jesus, to die in our place.

He did not do it just to keep us from going to hell. He did it because He longs for us to draw closer to Him. When a person invites Jesus into their heart, the Father invites them into His heart. Listen to how the Father longs for us to pursue Him: "O my dove, that art in the clefts of the rock, in the secret places of the stairs, let me see thy countenance, let me hear thy voice; for sweet is thy voice, and thy countenance is comely" (Song of Sol. 2:14). How He longs for us to draw nearer to Him. There will be times when He will waken us in the night, longing for fellowship. I have had Him awaken me early in the morning, well before the sun is up, to just come and spend time with Him. It is hard for us to fathom that the Father—the Creator of the universe—enjoys hearing our voice! I know this is a crude example, but remember how excited you were when you got your first puppy or kitten? You loved playing with it. When it was sleeping, you would wait there, watching and waiting for it to wake up so you could resume your play. This is similar to the way the Father responds. He watches over us, waiting for the moment we awaken and acknowledge Him! The Father loves to hear our voice and our songs!

We read, "I sleep, but my heart waketh: it is the voice of my beloved that knocketh, saying, Open to me, my sister, my love, my dove, my undefiled: for my head is filled with dew, and my locks with the drops of the night" (Song of Sol. 5:2). There will be times while at work or at home when the Spirit will prompt you to stop what you are doing and get alone with Him. It is important that you are obedient during those times. I have found from personal experience that the Father can be grieved if we neglect to spend time with Him when He calls. I cannot explain why He sometimes chooses times like the early morning or when we are in the middle of doing something to want us to commune with Him. Perhaps just to see if we will choose to spend time with Him. Maybe it is to test the level of our love for Him. When we dated, wouldn't we do almost anything for our beloved? We would stay up late talking on the phone, or get up early to talk and get the day started with them. Why is it so different for our Lord? One day at work as I walked into the restroom to wash my apple, the Lord said, "I love you." It was so clear and real that I smiled and replied, "I love you too, Lord."

There are times when He will speak to us through dreams and visions. The more time we spend with Him, the more in tune we become to His voice. Jesus said that His sheep would know and recognize His voice. Please understand that I am talking about a real relationship with the Father; it is not something strange or unreal. Some people actually think that once they get close to the Father they will lose touch with reality (as they understand reality to be) and end up being so heavenly minded they are of no earthly good. That, of course, is not true. Touching God's heart will only cause us to excel in our walk as Christians. It is true that we will care less and less for this world as we spend time in His presence. Things just will not have the pull on us that they did before. The reason that happens is because nothing here on earth can make us feel the way we feel when we are lost in God's presence.

As we pursue God, our prayers will become less selfish and more Christ-centered. We will come to a place in our walk where we are more concerned with what He thinks than what others think. Our decisions will be based not so much on the impact they have on us, but on the impact they have on our relationship with Him. Any separation of that relationship would be rejected, and thus not given another thought.

A love that strong is the result of building a relationship over time—and is worth the pursuit. As the scripture says, "Many waters cannot quench love, neither can the floods drown it" (Song of Sol. 8:7). There is so much the Father longs to share with us. We need to also guard against taking our relationship with the Father for granted. We must hold as precious our relationship with Him and the things He shares with us.

As the river of His presence begins flowing in your life, it will eventually touch other lives, too. You may be the catalyst to revival in your church. Hungry people birth hunger in others. I get no greater joy than in leading someone to

Christ, and then seeing him or her long to enter into His presence. We must make up our minds that nothing will deter us from seeking after the heart of God. I want to see Him in every church, taking over the services and leading the people into His presence. So many people do not realize what they are missing. They are so caught up in their lives and what this world has to offer them. It breaks God's heart to see His children spend more time doing what makes them feel good than in entertaining Him. It is not that going out and having fun is wrong, but our relationship with Him must be first. It must be central to everything else. We should plan our lives around Him, rather than trying to plan God around our lives. This takes effort and a purposeful pursuit. A hungry person will not be denied! There will be people who do not understand your pursuit or passion for Him. Some will even mock you; but such is the attitude of those who are content to live in the outer court. I would not trade my relationship with the Father or my passionate pursuit of Him for anything. I have not obtained the closeness I desire, and I still feel that I am only waist deep in the river of His presence; yet I sense that He is drawing me out to deeper waters. I have vowed to pursue a nearness with the Father until, like Moses before me, I feel His breath on my cheek. Even then I will look into His face, give Him all my love and say, "Father, take me deeper into the depths of Your presence. I want more of You!"

The Father is about to repossess His church. We were birthed in power, and we will go out in power. Our churches should be places of refuge and restoration, which is the result of the members pursuing Him in their individual lives throughout the week, not just when they walk through the door of a church. The writer of Habakkuk said, "For the earth shall be filled with the knowledge of the glory of the LORD, as the waters cover the sea" (Hab. 2:14). The day is coming when the earth will be filled with the understanding and knowledge of His weighty manifest presence. How will people come to understand that? When hungry people like you and me come from His presence and tell others of His desire for them to draw closer. I am waiting for that day when we will walk into church and our praise and worship will be such that the heavens are rent, and He will come down and abide in our midst. Paul said, "For ye were sometimes darkness, but now are ye light in the Lord: walk as children of light" (Eph. 5:8). Every time you catch a glimpse of the manifest presence of God or His glory, it is described as light or fire or lightning. He calls us children of light because not only is Christ alive in us, but the closer we get to Him the more He shines in and through us. I believe the reason God sometimes shows up in our services is because the reflection of His Son is as bright in our lives as we are worshiping Him and He has to come check it out personally! God told me one time, "Before heaven will kiss earth, you must first kiss Me."

How hungry are you? Do you really long for Him more than anything else in your life? You determine how close you come to Him. On His part, He is more than willing to share His life and love with us. The level and intensity of my hunger for God will determine the level and depth of my communion and intimacy with Him. I believe that He will restore His glory back to the church as the Word declares.

The restoration of the relationship that the Father had in the Garden of Eden means our closeness to Him should be the norm, not the exception. We, as Christians, have become satisfied with knowing either about God or knowing Him from a distance. Perhaps the reason for this is because the closer we get, the more vulnerable we become. We cannot hide anything from the Father. Sometimes we think we can, but the closer we get, the more He will lead us to the laver to show us what He sees. I cannot judge others, or question their closeness to God; I can only encourage them to draw nearer, and keep my own relationship hot after Him. Each person is as close to God as they want to be.

Keep in mind that the things God reveals to us are entirely up to Him; we cannot manipulate the Spirit of the Lord. His perfect will for us is to get as close as we possibly can. And keep in mind that those He rejects are those at the end who did not accept Him or know Him intimately. Jesus said there would be a time when He would say to those who rejected Him to depart. He said in Matthew 7:23, "And then will I profess unto them, I never knew you: depart from me, ye that work iniquity." The word for *knew* in the Greek means "did not know intimately." I believe on that day His heart will be pained as He turns people away. He did not give His best in order to have a distant bride; therefore, we need to draw near to the honeymoon suite, the secret place, for intimate communion with our Lord, our Lover, Jesus Christ!

Will you make Him the Lover of your soul? The Father longs so much for you to find the joy of touching His heart. My prayer for you is that your desire and hunger for Him will far surpass and exceed every other desire you have. Do not delay any longer! Right where you are, stop whatever you are doing, and look to Him and pray:

> *Father, how I long to feel Your heartbeat as John did. How I long to walk with You as Abraham did. How I long to hear You call me Your friend. Show me Your glory as You did Moses. I cry out to You as Paul did, that I might know You. I long to have a heart after You like Your servant David had, Father. I am tired of going to church and tasting of Your presence, then ignoring You the rest of the week. I want You, Father, more than Your gifts and blessings. I want to see Your face. I long for Your touch. I won't stop seeking You or desiring to feel Your heartbeat until I feel Your breath on my cheek. Even then, Father, I will look up at You and say that I want more, that I'm not satisfied. I'm still hungry for You!*

If you really mean that, you will not be disappointed. The Holy Spirit told me to tell everyone reading this book whose prayer and desire is to draw closer to Him, "I will answer their prayer. I will answer the longing of their heart. I will draw them to Me." Don't you feel His tugging? He longs for you to come before Him, face to face, beyond the veil.

About the author:

Jesse Wilson was born and raised in Petoskey, Michigan. When he was in his teens his parents moved to a small town about ten miles away where they began attending a small Pentecostal church. It was while he was living in that small town of 500 people, Alanson, Michigan, that he gave his heart to God in his late teens. After graduating from high school he attended Jimmy Swaggart Bible College. After spending a year in college he felt led to move to Tampa, Florida, where he became an assistant pastor of his future father-in-law's church. Jesse was married to Charity Skiles in June 1991, and in 1995 they left the church to pioneer an independent church. In 1997 they and their two children, Caleb and Jessica, moved from Tampa to Zephyrhills and have been members of Celebration Family Church for over six years working in various ministry outreaches. Jesse has earned an associate of theology degree from Life School of Ministry and has ministered in churches in Florida, Michigan, Missouri, and Alabama. His wife, Charity, is currently the praise and worship leader at their home church.

To contact the author:

If you would like to contact Jesse for speaking engagements or conferences, you may reach him at his home church:

Celebration Family Church

Office phone: (813) 782-2888
Fax: (813) 788-1530

Or write Jesse at:

Passionate Pursuit Ministries

P.O. Box 901
Zephyrhills, FL 33539-0901